THE ROAD TO

REVIEWS

"The sequence in which you describe your childhood experiences and simultaneously explain the impacts they had on you is very engaging. The way in which you revealed the events was deeply enlightening. Very profound work. Well done.!"
—Trevor Opio, Reader

"The book made me go into the shoes of the writer and yet feeling that somehow I may have been in the same situation at some points in my life in a different context. The vivid storytelling of his experiences helped me as a primary school teacher understand on another's point of view how my pupils would be suffering at their tender age".
—Jayine Ocampo, Educator

'Exceptionally written, highly motivational and thought provoking read! With the writers perspective vivid in your mind and truly captivating you by leading you through his journey, intertwined with messages of hope and endearing persistence, he's telling you of the raw while showing you the strength it's taken. This book truly shows the power of taking control of your mental health journey and never giving up!'
—Kaitlyn Walker, Reader

THE ROAD TO MENTAL WELLNESS

Jonathan Arenburg

*written for therapeutic release,
published in the hopes it will help others*

The Road to Mental Wellness
Copyright ©2021 Jonathan Arenburg
Berwick, Nova Scotia

ISBN: 978-1-7778799-0-7
September 2021

Editor:
Winnie Czulinski

Front cover design and photo:
Angelina Obritsch, Average Jane Photography

Formatter:
Catherine A. MacKenzie
www.writingwicket@gmail.com

All Rights Reserved.
No portion of this publication may be reproduced, stored in any electronic system, or transmitted in any form or by any means, electronic, mechanical, photocopy, recording, or otherwise without written permission from the author.

Kenzie —

much Love for your mental Health

[signature]

To my mom, dad and my sister:
from the beginning, you
were the ever-present lights
that guided me through my life...
Love you!

FOREWORD
by Stephen Schneider

Having worked for many years as a criminologist, my awareness of mental health issues is unfortunately all too often viewed through the prism of the criminal justice system – and what I have learned is not too encouraging. The police seem to have become this country's first responders to those experiencing mental health crises while our correctional system appears to be the central government institution through which a disproportionate number of people suffering from mental health and substance abuse disorders are housed.

Many of those who come into contact with the criminal justice system seek treatment, but the services are frequently not available. Others refuse to turn for help for fear that their behaviours will be criminalized.

Still others are reluctant to admit they may have a problem due to the social stigma that has long been attached to mental health and substance abuse disorders. This is especially true among men, who seem to put machismo and other outwardly masculine traits ahead of their self-care.

That is why I so admire and applaud Jonathan who, in this new book, not only displays the courage to admit his struggle with anxiety, depression and PTSD, but to put himself out there (through both his book and blog) to share his story, bring attention to these issues, and help ease any stigma that others in similar positions may be feeling.

Indeed, through this story Jonathan has personalized the experiences of many people struggling with mental health issues and in doing so has created a forum, and indeed a safe space, for others to come forward and tell their own story and begin their own healing process.

In his highly personable, but literary writing style, Jonathan narrates his journey from childhood to adolescence to adulthood. His story is familiar; he is forced to run the gamut of personal and social environmental risk factors: family breakup and neglect, sadness, loneliness, feelings of helplessness, self-isolation, bullying, and the pressure to fit in.

His childhood reminiscences about the onset of his mental health problems highlight one of the issues that I have long advocated for: a more preventative approach to adolescent and adult mental health problems by addressing their root causes early in the life of a child.

Far too often we see the early warning signs during childhood but write them off as temporary. Parents and other caregivers can be willfully blind to symptoms of stress and anxiety, deal with them through harsh or inconsistent punishment or simply hope they dissipate with maturity. Worse, the children most in need are often denied timely access to assessment and treatment services or are misdiagnosed.

Notwithstanding the need for an early diagnosis and treatment, many of us have the personal resilience that helps weather the storms that come with mental health problems. For Jonathan, his intelligence, compassion for others, and commitment to public service (reflected in his career choices, whether as a fire fighter, a counsellor, or a support worker) have no doubt helped him cope.

It is these selfless qualities that perhaps constitute a life force that keeps Jonathan going, to share his story, and to prompt others to be introspective and unafraid to admit they have "a problem" and may need help from others.

Jonathan's story reminds us that we define ourselves by the choices we make; our lives are, in fact, the sum of our choices. Events unfold so quickly and so unjustly at times, that human happiness does not appear to be included in the design of our lives or our society. It is only our human capacity to be self-aware, compassionate, and loving that gives meaning to the chaotic and indifferent universe. At the very least, Jonathan has helped us understand our little corner of the universe and how we can change it and ourselves for the better.

Stephen Schneider, Ph.D.,
Professor, Department of Criminology,
Saint Mary's University,
Nova Scotia, Canada.

CONTENTS

Prologue 1

Chapter One 3
Monster Precursor for Illness

Chapter Two 19
Perception isn't Always Reality

Chapter Three 26
Hitting High School and Experiencing Sad Realities

Chapter Four 37
The Road Toward Mental Illness

Chapter Five 47
Moving Towards Normalcy

Chapter Six 58
The Real World

Chapter Seven 64
Breaking Point

Chapter Eight 69
Finally, a Glimmer of Normality

Chapter Nine 77
What Exactly Went Wrong?

Chapter Ten.. 88
Conquering the Mountain

Chapter Eleven... 98
The Buck Doesn't Stop There

Chapter Twelve 105
My Triumphant Comeback

Chapter Thirteen 114
My Dreams Realized

Chapter Fourteen 137
My New Life, Definitely Not a Fairy Tale

Chapter Fifteen 150
A Not So Happy Thanksgiving

Chapter Sixteen 157
Losing My Grip

Chapter Seventeen 165
Into the Abyss

Chapter Eighteen 176
Finally, a Glimmer of Normality

Chapter Nineteen 185
Rescue the Rescuer

About the Author 193

Connect with the Author 194

PROLOGUE

There was a day – not long before I finished this book and sent it bumping towards the production pipeline – that I was feeling really quite good, at peace. And it was when I was going to end my life. If I had, obviously, there'd be no book in your hands now, or at least a very different one, cobbled together by a co-writer, a colleague, a friend.

What, you might wonder, makes someone want to end their life? When there's the feeling of "enough is enough." But not just in a vague, everyday kind of way. It was as if I was drowning, and could barely move my feet. I'd also seen and done things in my life – as a firefighter and first responder – no one should have to see. And I've had some terrifying and flat-line-depressing experiences. Over and over. I've also been a counsellor, helping others with major issues like depression, PTSD and addictions abuse. I know they have depended on me at times, and it has meant the world to me to help people, as I've always been moved to do. But now their "rescuer" has had it.

So...heading out to end my life. As the details at the end of this book show, I took steps to prepare myself...for what? Useful items to take with me in case I didn't do "the deed," and found all I needed was some little refuge away from home. That's the way suicide thoughts sometimes go, back and forth, up and down.

And sometimes when you decide to end it all – personally I can speak only for myself – you get this really good feeling. Anyone seeing me toss my backpack into my brand new 2021 Toyota Corolla Hybrid might have thought I was going off on some pleasure jaunt. I'm sure I was even smiling. Now, just think about this. It could be that some of those people – young men, women, all folks – who look peacefully happy while they pack up their car with personal belongings, might be going off to meet death.

And I'd had this car for only a few weeks. A waste, you might think? Not necessarily, if I could manage to do "it" in a way that didn't mar the car, even if it made a mess of me. Anyway...I found myself driving along, singing one of George Michael's ballads about being loved. *Loooooved.* And then I had a crash...and hit something. But this wasn't the way I'd planned it. And it shook me up so much, even for just a minute or two, that I felt, I swear, some of the proverbial life flash before my eyes. The life I'd meant to end. The life I'd lived for forty-odd years. The life that was taken over, now and then, by a monster, two monsters. Depression and PTSD (post-traumatic stress disorder).

Maybe you suffer from this yourself, maybe you know someone who does, maybe you know nothing but are willing to find out...and maybe you're a professional who would welcome a full-fledged account from one guy pumped full of medications, therapists and (mis)diagnoses.

Join me for this ride. It may help you see why I'd decided to take that "final ride" – the one that didn't quite work out as I'd planned. And that, I figure, is for a reason. Because my time here is not done yet.

I've got too much to do. Maybe because of all my blogging, podcasts, counselling, posting – and now this book and I hope others – I've been called an Influencer.

Proper job description or not, I'll take it. The process of getting there was a long one, and it's ongoing. And I hope it has meaning for your own journey. We are on that journey together.

"No matter how dark our days are, fighting for your life means that you search for any sliver of light, any sign to keep going on your own road to mental wellness."

Jonathan Arenburg

CHAPTER ONE

Monster Precursor for Illness

"What they didn't understand, is that behaviour always happens for a reason and that reason. What is the acting-out behaviour really telling us?"

It's difficult to say when my dance with the mental-illness devil began. I think back to being around four years old, when I had this thing about holding the doors open for people. It was almost like a contest with myself to see how much I could do it and how helpful I could be. "I will, I will!" But now I'm wondering if I was opening the door to something terrible, dark and unseen, something that would almost destroy my life – and certainly change it forever.

And it was invisible. I'm sure that had I been able to see it, I would have slammed the door shut, even at four years old. If it had claws, a long scaly tail, terrible teeth, angry eyes, mouth breathing stinking fire...yes, I like to think that even at that tender age, my instinct would have been to stop it coming in.

Jump forward a few years. Since I was the age of seven or eight, I could feel this presence dancing around in my highly-sensitive head, moulding me slowly by hijacking my thoughts and altering the way I experienced the world. I am convinced that this is the reason I believed in the boogieman. He didn't reside under my bed but instead, he took up real estate in the recesses of my mind.

My naive perception of the world started to crumble at the age of five, when I first walked into my local kindergarten class sporting a navy-blue backpack with bright red trim and rocking a pair of Converse Fast Break sneakers, the best of the 1980s.

If I had any love for school at all, it ended on that very first day when my teacher gently explained to me: "No, John. You must leave your book-bag in this cubby, the one with your name on it." What? It was a stained and lacquered thing I hated.

That was when I had my Snoopy-like meltdown, head thrown back, tears springing from my eyes. "No, no, no!" I can picture it now, sun streaming through the window, making it even harder to see. That kind of grief, upset and protest came out in childhood more through tears. I didn't know how to do it in any other way.

It would be a long road I travelled on, before I knew – much later – what it was like to be the young man who smashed his fists into rock-hard cinder-block walls and solidly-constructed fire doors. That's what mental illness can be like, and that's what much of this story is about, the whole journey to getting there

And beyond such physical memories, I know what it's like for others to want to dump me, to offload their "problem," me, on to another school. True, it was a transfer, though I did switch schools for high school.

And then it would be another path from there, to becoming a firefighter. I would see things no human should see, travelling on a narrow road with flames all around me and death facing me each time I went out. Time and again. The potential of death, destruction, buildings raging and then smouldering ruins. Charred remains, and not only of buildings. Can you imagine how that kind of thing eventually would force a face-to-face meeting with PTSD (post-traumatic stress disorder)? It would add itself to the problem that came out in much earlier years and would make it just that much more potent.

Along the way, I became successful at managing my mental illness. So I thought. In fact, I was so convinced I had defeated my demons, that I stopped going to counselling. I would suffer the consequences. Why didn't I see the disaster that was slowly unfolding inside of me? Maybe because I didn't want to believe it?

Mental illness walked alongside me, constantly conjuring up worst-case scenarios in my ear. I was able to put distance between myself and my severe anxiety, so that the anxious voice was a dim holler way off in the distance. That voice had so little power that I stopped paying attention. A colossal mistake, and one I would pay for.

However, this is also a story of relative success and comeback. The ride we are going on is one that in the end leads also to face-to-face meeting with survival, helping others, and helping myself.

My overt sensitivity turned me into a grade-school tuning fork. I felt every little shift in the moods of entire groups of people if the room was thick with stress or the air was made still by sadness. It made me feel as though I was in some sort of mentally-made boxing ring and the vibes from the environment were its blows to the face. I felt it all and felt it intensely, no matter where I went.

Being as young as I was, I had no idea why I was blessed or cursed with this sensitivity. In my naivety, I simply thought this was the way everyone experienced the world. "Just the way it is." Not so. I would later learn that certain people are predisposed to being more sensitive than others and don't just mosey through the world around them, but feel it as they go. A fact I wish I was armed with in my youth. Perhaps I would have somehow been better able to handle what I was experiencing, not only externally but internally. My life at home was not immune to my finely-tuned wiring. It's as though someone threw a train into motion and then snapped off the brake switch, with this highly-sensitive disposition never shut off.

This reverberating force that dominated and shaped who I was becoming was like a double-edged sword. At the time I didn't know its impact on my personality and my mental health, but it was the foundation for who I was then and would become over the course of my lifetime. This disorder would keep intruding, as it's known to, and insert itself into my daily living, leaving controversy and hardship strewn along my life's path like leaves gone bad.

The wonderful thing about this highly-sensitive personality trait is that – as I have found – it produces huge amounts of empathy for others. Because I had absolutely no idea that this trait was even a thing growing up, I didn't question where this empathic sensor came from. It simply picked up on others' pain and I instinctively knew that people were in emotional distress.

"You are hurting, you need something," I would mumble to myself, directed at them. I might not always have been sure of what it was they needed but I felt compelled to ask. Some were understandably reluctant, so I would always offer up "I'm here if you ever need someone to listen."

In a kind of superhero sense, a warm sympathetic feeling would wash over me and cause me to gravitate towards those suffering. It was almost like the "hero's cloak," used for good.

For as long as I can remember I have reached out to help others and have always loved it. Even if this may sound – yeah – too self-admiring, I believe that this compassionate aspect of who I was has made me into the person I am today: caring, in a professional and personal sense. And being in tune with others on an emotional level was a likely driver for my tendency to take things hard.

It would take me years, but I would come to understand that "My God – sensitivity and mental illness are like fire and gasoline." They made any pain I felt much more intense, and because they were constantly being mixed together, the two would engulf me on a near-constant basis.

I believe that this behavioural "wiring" propelled me to love more authentically. As far back as I can remember, I "got" the importance of family. It may be a function of this wiring, but it may also have to do with my mother having a large family, possibly both. I have many fond memories of being at my grandparents' Christmas get-togethers. It was wall-to-wall relatives, shouting and laughing over top of one another, every room full of cigarette smoke and goodies of all shapes and sizes arranged as though a professional caterer had nothing better to do on Christmas Eve. "Get over here for your dessert!" We sang Christmas carols and played cards by the fire. "Who's up for making a card house and a good round of Rummy?"

We kids would run and go so hard all night, our ears burning. We were so hot and tired, but we always went the distance and stayed awake for the entire time. It was the most magical time of my life. And once we arrived home, I felt the magic of our four-person family. There was a warmth running through me making me feel as though no harm could ever come to us, or the world for that matter. I have always wanted this feeling as an adult but alas, it has never materialized like it did on those beautiful family-focused Christmases and other family gatherings.

Looking back on my early childhood, I recall I was always told "John, you have a big heart." This seemingly good-hearted nature I was gifted with amplified those warm and wonderful moments with family, and for that I will always be grateful. My momma always said I was "Such a sweet little boy, always doing for others." Often, she would say, even to this day, "When you were little, you were always smiling and always so happy."

As far back as I can remember, I was holding open doors and smiling at the people who walked through them. I found joy in the warm smiles and polite greetings I received in return. I treasure what seems to be a built-in compassion option that comes with this life package I was given. But as with all great things, there is a rotten consequence for possessing such abilities.

As I grew into these presumably inherited traits, I began to feel the sting of being a sensitive, compassionate and easy-going child. It's true what they say, ignorance is bliss. When you're four or five years old, the world as you know it is near perfect – well, except for the meltdowns from pure exhaustion and the occasional "No!" from Mom or Dad when you're asking for a toy. Other than that, my early years were pretty much Utopian.

My naive perception of the world started to crumble at the age of five, when I first walked into that local kindergarten class, my feet securely in those hip 1980s sneakers, my back embraced by that navy-blue backpack with bright red trim.

This was the first day I can recall feeling the darker side of sensitivity. Upon learning that I would be separated from the backpack that I loved (because it made me feel like a big kid), I had that meltdown. Like Snoopy when devastated over any number of things, I threw my head back and the tears started flowing. I felt a deep sense of sadness, a sadness that lingered perhaps longer than it should have. If I recall correctly, despite the chaos running through me, the teacher got her way.

The Emergence of Sadness

Before I set off on my new adventure that was "big school," there was a series of things that took place in my young life that may have started the mudslide of depression. This would manifest itself in or about grade three or four. Being too young, in preschool days, to understand the complexities of being overly sensitive, I still got the harsh realities of life. It would turn out or seem to me that from the day of my birth, my life was fraught with challenges.

First, my emergence into this world was a turbulent and precarious one. Born in an Ontario hospital in the mid-1970s, I greeted doctors with two legs black and blue, and was unresponsive. As the story goes, I was whisked away and three minutes later, my sister made her way into the world, both healthy and vocal.

Fortunately, the medical teams were able to successfully revive me, and as a result I was granted an amazing gift, life. My sister and I were born a month premature and in a time when medicine was nowhere near as sophisticated as it is today.

Although I have no personal recollection of my experience, I still feel a huge sense of gratitude as a result of it. Looking back on the odds that I would survive is remarkable to me. This story of how I was first introduced into the world helps ground me in troubled times. Locked deep within the neural pathways of my brain (as a therapist might say), there it lies. I think that this is why I have been able to "feel" when I recall it. It's a powerful force, that produces real, genuine gratitude for being granted an opportunity to live.

Perhaps my early years are what drive me to find the key to a cure for my troubled mind today. Could it be my brush with death has a role to play in the disintegration of my mental health? The scientific part of me often wonders what an impact my turbulent entrance into the world had on me. What impact did my emergence into the world have, deprived of oxygen as I was? I may never know the answer, but it will always be a nagging question.

After living in an incubator for the best part of three months, and one surgery later, I had a procedure to remove the toes – except for the big one – on my right foot. Somehow the surgeons thought this might clear up the black and blue that ran the entire length of my baby legs. The decision came down to amputating my toes or both of my legs. Fortunately, the left leg showed signs of improvement, the discolouration slowly faded, and the pink hue of newborn skin started to dominate.

From this revelation, they elected to take the toes, a decision that changed my little life forever. The significant impact of potentially losing my legs has never been lost on me – who knows what path my life would have taken had this become my reality? This fateful decision is another reason I will always appreciate the gift of life and always fight to keep it.

With six toes in total and both legs the colour mother nature intended them to be, I was sent home to finally be reunited with my mother and sister. My biological father, noticeably missing from the story, was not involved in our lives. A guitar-playing band member with long brown hair and riddled with anxiety himself, he had met my mother at a bar he played at. A man with another family. My mother realized that this was a scenario she didn't want for us. It wasn't as though he didn't want to be involved. There were simply too many dynamics in play to allow for it.

Eleven months after my sister and I were born, we found ourselves on a plane and touching down in my mother's home province of Nova Scotia. I suppose my mother felt this was the best thing for us all, to create distance between us and the potential hardships that would have come out of staying. Now, as an adult, I believe it was the best decision she could have made. And it would influence what became my life's journey.

And the Sadness Continues...

Only a few years later, when we were three, my sister fell ill and was hospitalized for a long period of time. My mom, on her own, had tons of stressful things on her plate: a very sick little gal, a young lad whose needs – emotional, physical and otherwise – had to be met, and on top of that, she was unsupported by family with the exception of her father. He supported her in secret because he knew it would open a Pandora's box of trouble had any of his ten other children found out.

There seemed to be a streak of resentment through my mom's family at the time, a disdain for one another. Maybe it was the size of the family or how family issues were managed over its history. Whatever the case, there was a huge rift, one the remaining members would attempt to fix in their later years.

My mother was a woman whose passion and wisdom were so intense that she took zero garbage from anyone. Her expressive nature, although mostly proved to indicate the true and accurate, turned her into the black sheep of the family. The pain she felt on a daily basis was way more than I could ever bear. How lonely and isolating that must have been for her, to not only be abandoned by her family, but to be a constant source of bullying and ridicule from those who were supposed to love and support her. All that controversy, with a toddler in the hospital with an uncertain future! Unimaginable. She would later tell me, "I have no idea how I got through those days. But I did."

I, on the other hand – and oblivious to the constant bombardment of my mother's family battles and her challenges as a single mom scraping by – was in heaven. The entire time my sister was in hospital I spent every waking moment with my mom, even tagging along to her workplace. She worked in an office as a receptionist/bookkeeper. I did whatever toddlers do when they are stuck within the confines of their mother's workplace. What I can remember is playing out in the yard there from time to time.

"I'm here, Mom is here," I would sing to myself as I enjoyed the yard and its patches of mud.

I can't recall much more about this period of time, memories lost to the years like accumulating sands over an ancient ruin. This whole period of my life seems eroded by the passage of time and as a result, not much of it remains in my head. Still, it left an indelible mark on the rest of my life's journey.

Being so young, both my sister and I could not possibly have understood the complexities of what was taking place. Nor could we ever hope to comprehend the pain and sacrifice our mother was making. All I knew was that my little sister, younger by three minutes, was in hospital, that it was serious, and that this little brunette-haired girl had to go it alone. Why? Because Mom's support system was so sparse that there was just no way she could stay by her strong little girl's side as much as she wanted to. I can't imagine the pain in both the hearts of my beautiful, kind-hearted twin sister and my very strong and wonderfully independent mother.

Thankful to say, and much to the relief of my mother, my sister made a full recovery and came home to be reunited with her family. I'm sure she was happy to be home and no longer suffering in her sadness over being left in a dimly-lit hospital room with the faint smell of disinfectant in the air and only thin bed sheets to keep her warm throughout the night. Being left alone in that bland and sterile environment affected her. Being as young as she was, her only response was that of anger. "I hate you!" she would say to Mom. "I don't want to be here. I want to go home!"

Finally, it was a family of three back together again and a little bleached-blond-haired boy happy to see his sister. "Yay!

Love you!" We attempted to move on with our lives and put this very uncertain time behind us. But for me, this happiness would fade quickly when I realized I would have to split my mother's time with my sister. You may think I was acting spoiled and selfish, and maybe that's what it looked like, but as a child of that age, I did not have much understanding of the whole scenario.

As time moved on and life settled into normality, I felt increasingly sad and lonely. "Help me," I would say – but I had no idea who could. I was still that loving little kid with a big heart, but somehow, some way, that toddler-sized heart had been damaged in ways it would take years for me to understand.

As I look back on it now, I can feel how the intensity that comes with my sensitive nature amplified this lonely and sad feeling, to the degree that it latched on to me. I have been its host, its means of survival, ever since. I now know that this sadness and loneliness manifested into depression and anxiety. To this day, it's unclear to me why those feelings of abandonment had such an impact. In some senses it seems so disproportionate. Regardless, the feelings of abandonment would be a theme that kept playing, like a stuck piece of equipment, throughout my life.

Only a few years later, my stepfather would walk into our lives and change it forever. It was a moment in my life I will always be grateful for, but it would further divide my time with my mother. It was sort of like "Hello, Dad. Goodbye, Mom." It's clear that this further dissection of Mom's time had an impact on my feeling of loneliness, and it was overshadowed by the fact I now had a dad.

The Manifestation of Mental Illness

In the adventure that was school, as far as I recall it, the first few years of my public education were unremarkable. But I am certain the feelings of loneliness were boiling just under the surface of this grade-schoolboy's young smile. Maybe it was my insatiable desire for exploration and play that kept it all in check. Like many children of the eighties, I was obsessed with Transformers. They occupied a lot of space in my head. As a result, I would allow my imagination to take over. They were my world at times – yet there was another world trying to claim me.

I recall the main struggle starting to show itself around grade four when I encountered my first undesirable teacher. A wiry little lady with an early version of Harry Potter-like glasses and the floaty, flowered fashion sense of the nineteen-sixties, she had a hurried-ness about her, and seemingly was always on a mission.

My grade-four year started off with a book-bag full of school supplies and uncertainty. I recall the classroom well. Sprawled across the floor was a purple industrial rug, wooden-paned windows from the early years of the 20th century, and a small man-door in the back. I took a seat in the back at one of the many round tables, and there I remained for the year. I don't know why I chose the back. I do remember feeling "safer" although at the time I'm not sure what I was afraid of. I can say now that it was likely anxiety trickling to the surface. Or maybe it was the empathic sensor warning me of the energy present in the room.

By the time I landed in this woman's classroom, I was struggling to grasp the concept of math, and failed to see any real use for a lot of the material being taught. I would toss my homework away on the walk home from school – "Who needs it?" I'd say to myself – and make what I thought was a convincing argument that I had lost it. I soon learned that this scheme to get out of homework was no good. The teacher quickly caught on.

I felt, even then, that these two factors made up her mind that I was a write-off, and to be de-prioritized. I felt picked on. No, that's an understatement. It left me feeling as though the very scalp of my identity had been yanked off. She seemed to take a kind of sour glee in seeing me squirm. Whatever her motivation, the feelings of loneliness and sadness stirred within me with each passing day, till finally sadness just overtook me. But rather then expressing it to the outside world as what I was feeling – sadness – it exploded out of me, as anger. Hated that teacher, hated life, hated myself.

It boiled and bubbled to the surface at full speed, and I was too young and not skilled enough to understand why I was so angry. My emotions took possession of my heart, and my mouth engaged long before my brain. I developed a hair-trigger temper, and it ruled me to the degree that by halfway through the year I was blowing up on a regular basis.

But why? What was it about this year that finally caused the volcano that was my long-pressurized sadness to finally let go? Honestly, I believe I was depressed and lonely for far too long. And this shrill-voiced, seemingly stressed teacher was, well, just mean and scary, and ensured that the table I chose at the beginning of the year, the one in the back, was where I stayed. I guess my young heart could no longer stand the lonely, marginalized realm of being alone…I guess it was just too much.

Sometimes I wonder if the flames of my anger were fuelled by a familiar feeling I experienced back in the days when my sister came home from the hospital. Sadness seemed always to be the common denominator.

This temper, fed by a deep sense of isolation cultivated by this teacher, grew in its ferocity, like that of a monster in a movie, a gargantuan-sized beast, whom I have always imagined was as black as it was huge. A beast that seemed to stand at my side, always weighing me down with dread and fear.

It seemed to grow off the life force of others and as a result, it became almost unstoppable. Before the year's end, my internal struggle escalated to the degree of physical outburst. Because of this escalation, my poor ten-year-old fists began to crash into walls and other inanimate objects as my mental pain became too much for its container. When I was filled to the brim, it was as if the unidentified turmoil housed within my child-sized vessel cried out "I gotta be released!"

By the time I had reached this crossroad, I had felt the sting of loneliness for most of my young life. But it wasn't only the turmoil at school that triggered my feelings of abandonment. My home life generally was met with the sound of silence at the door when I got home. "Hello?" I would say. "Hello?" There was just silence, even an echo.

My mother and father were the hardest-working people I have ever known. Dad, a country man raised on fishing and hunting, spent the majority of his time plugging away at his one true love – his work. A truly gifted carpenter, he was gone day and night, home just long enough to eat, sleep and make his lunch in the morning.

My mother, having two jobs for what seemed to be the better part of our lives, was home only long enough to make supper, then off again to help her father in his exceptionally large vegetable garden, or help him mow or paint. "Busy, John!" she would say to my mouth full of food as I tried to talk. She spent her working days as a sharp-as-a-tack bookkeeper for two companies and when the weekend rolled around, it was more painting, mowing and cleaning, this time at our place. The family times that I had craved all those years were few and far between and, well, it affected me greatly. "Mom...Dad..." I wanted to say. "Can't we do something together?"

Now, though, I don't blame them for their long absences, and see they were very much a product of their time. They believed that working hard to provide for their family was the most important thing they could do for us. I admire them for that and will always be grateful for their hard, honest work that put clothes on my back and food on the table. I treasure them, as a lifelong gift.

When I reflect on this period of my life, I realize now that the darker forces that consumed me as a child likely were that of depression. My folks were only doing what they believed to be the best way to live and to raise their children. "Can we go to a restaurant and eat?" This was met with "No, we are too busy."

Every now and then, I would ask my dad, "Can we throw the baseball around?" It happened once and I don't think he enjoyed it. Although we were spending time together, his mind was still focused on his work. It never happened again.

I can literally count on one hand the amount of times we had done "dad and the lad" activities. One that sticks out is when we went fishing together when I was nine. We went to a local river. I was not interested but wanted to spend time with him, so I gladly went. It all went downhill when he realized that my nine-year-old legs couldn't jump across to the other side. His solution? To grab my arm and fling me across the rapidly-running water. The force of his throw was successful – however, I landed on my face. That was enough for me to say "Never again."

In spite of their wonderful efforts, my pre-programmed sensitivity was at work. It came right out to intensify the sad, the lonely and the sense of abandonment. What I needed – some closeness – was the opposite of what I got. I see now that no one, not even me, knew to the degree that that was true. But like a well-watered plant, depression slowly took root and grew, slow and steady.

My First Encounter with Therapy

Just before I hit middle school, my behaviours were so awful and problematic that both my parents and my teachers were at a loss. The only times I experienced a reprieve from the plague that was helplessness was when I remember thinking to myself "I can't wait to get home and play the Nintendo N64." The imaginary world of Super Mario and Zelda give my brain a much-needed rest. It was because there was so much happening in *their* worlds, that imaginary world that became such a refuge for me.

My parents advocated for me. My mother's ferocious wisdom and her lion-like ability to stand her ground for not only herself, but also for her troubled son, ended up with her being able to recognize that this escalation was in need of some serious intervention. How many times did I hear her say, "That's it! That's it! We've got to do something. With you and with those teachers! They'll have to deal with *me*, John – me."

This resulted in many meetings with the school, ultimately ending up with an appointment to see someone at Mental Health. I can't recall if my preteen self opposed the idea of therapy or not. But I do know I felt grateful that my parents were able to try and understand what lay at the centre of my rage. "It's all right, John – you're going to be all right. There's something there we're trying to cope with, just like you are."

What actually happened during those sessions has been overwritten several times since I was a kid, leaving little to no memories of the actual sessions themselves. But I will never forget the gentle professional who helped me find answers. A tall, soft-spoken man from Egypt, he had a constant soothing tone of voice that was a refreshing break from all the noise and chaos of my life and the environment I was forced to trudge to every day for much of my life. Even just the way he said my name, "Jonathan," seemed to give me a shot of total relaxation, and all the tension seemed to melt away.

It didn't take long for his peaceful disposition to win me over, and as a result, it wasn't long before I earned his respect. He also said, "We have a rapport, John, and I want to help you uncover the source of your increase in these so-called undesirable behaviours." What I do remember from our many sessions of exploration was, as I said to him, these ever-present and often overpowering "feelings of sadness and abandonment."

His uncanny ability to keep me at ease and feel safe was to me his superpower. He really was like a gentle super-hero – and like any young boy, I'd grown up on tales and shows of caped crusaders. It could be that these feelings helped get me to a place where I began to understand why these acting-out behaviours arose. And both my family and I knew that deep within me there was this deep psychological wound that, even today, bleeds into my everyday life and runs over my opportunities to be happy.

When I think about the impact my parents have had on my life, I see their decision to put me in therapy was what you might call a defining moment. And it was something that would reverberate throughout my life. This moment was such a pinnacle. Its impact was, like the man who saved me, amazing.

CHAPTER TWO

Perception isn't Always Reality

"I was drowning. That's what it seems. I was struggling furiously while people looked on."

I knew how to get the attention of people, even if I didn't do it on purpose. Developing a temper and taking it out on the walls of the school got me noticed by the principal, the teachers – and the rest of junior-high. Around grade five, I developed a reputation that must have mirrored what everyone was observing. I was a "Bad Kid," one to avoid. And as a result, my isolation got worse, and my feelings of sadness and loneliness grew.

These episodes of anger, when they wore off, left me feeling ashamed and remorseful. It's like I would say to myself, "Are you in there?" looking for that other kid, that kind-hearted boy who came out, apologizing, and ready for the consequences. Such anger, such pain. I can remember hating this anger that was so deep-seeded, so ingrained into who I was that I had mistaken this pain for who I was as a person.

And the "kind, caring child – are you in there?" That kid who I had always been, gave in to this hatred. What does that mean? That my authentic self was a prisoner. It took on my identity, and I learned to really detest myself.

All my years through middle school I was a loner, in part because of what everyone around me saw. I can't blame them for keeping a distance. Violence in any form is scary, especially for children.

There was one classmate, a fair-haired guy, who became my friend. Together, we stuck to ourselves. We had a lot of things in common, our love for transformers being the biggest. These toys, these robots that could "transform" into vehicles and other objects had such a hold on us. "Autobot! Deception!" we'd yell out, depending on which side we were on. And maybe it was something that really appealed to me because it showed something could change suddenly, become so different.

Many of my childhood memories were forged at his house, a large century home with pink wooden siding on its exterior and a widow's peak – a railed rooftop platform – towering above the rest of the house. We would play in his room or large back yard for hours and hours. "I don't want to go home," I'd often say. There we were, getting lost in our collective imaginations the whole time. "Let's build! Let's go to war!" And as I soon felt, everything we were building was like a relief-valve. That cork had been stopping up years of pent-up pain.

"Thanks, buddy. Thanks for always being there for me," I say years later. I will always be grateful to him. My friend – one of the few things that made school bearable – helped provide a healthy outlet from the turmoil inside and gave me an opportunity to have something of a normal childhood. He just accepted and embraced me for who I was, and as a result our friendship flourished like one of those hardy many-leafed plants. I often think about where I would have ended up without this incredible bond. As an old TV song goes," Thank you for being a friend." Even though we were just kids, I can recall telling him that.

The only other outlet I had was getting lost within the active imagination of my own mind. When I was young, I spent most of my childhood at my grandparents.' They owned a huge property home. "Hi, hi, hi!" I would yell out. I was just giddy to be there. It was like my own personal fantasy amusement world. "This is Disneyland," I would say to myself, not caring who heard it. "My Disneyland."

The farmhouse was such a reassuring black-and-orange structure on the landscape. It had so many bedrooms every visit was a new adventure. The dilapidated old barn with worn wooden shingles, large sliding doors and metal roof, all less than two-hundred feet from the house, was like an echo chamber, and an amazing adventure every time I ran free in it. Some of the most fun I ever had was when I got lost in a singular play from its rock and dirt-floored basement to its old hay lofts.

But still, there was something going on in my brain I didn't know how to handle. All I knew was that I was angry. I obviously didn't have what the experts might call "skill sets," or any proper guidance. I always blamed other things – external forces, which I could even picture as some space-age thing – for my behaviors. "Here it comes, invading from outer space!" Where I seemed to exist much of the time was some weird landscape that might even have reassuring structures – like my grandparents' home – but way off in the distance.

I obviously didn't know what this inner pain really was. But I picture when I had candy, or was playing with sand or something, and watching it disappear – out of my grasp and falling into some black hole. My slipping through the cracks as a child has had a domino effect that is still in motion today.

Their Minds Were Made Up

I knew what they, the educational professionals with their make-believe psychologists' hats, were saying about me. "Yes...his problem behaviors are a direct result of some sort of learning disability."

What was it, exactly? I did have a proper learning assessment, where the evaluator said I was "a very bright child," but that I had some logistical things to overcome. My handwriting was one of them. My penmanship has always been a mess, chicken scratch, scribbles, illegible, you name it. Despite these results, they entered me into what they called a "general program, a program for those who can't keep pace with academic learning."

I can only figure their decision to downgrade my education was based on, partly, the echoes of my anger traveling down the narrow hallway of my small-town junior-high school.

I didn't understand what made the anger burn red-hot in me, but it was enough to make me feel like I was drowning in a sea of helplessness and frustration. So when the teachers and administration had concluded that I had "some sort of intellectual impairment" and my behaviors were a direct result, this stirred it up and took my suffering to a whole new level. How does a single student take on a system that was, by design, a teacher-student power imbalance?

I was drowning. That's what it seems. I was struggling furiously while people looked on, thinking and saying, "Just a kid being silly." They simply neglected to see or just didn't understand the seriousness of my situation. But I didn't understand it myself. What I really needed was their help – but didn't know how to say that.

A General Separation

For me, the title "General Education Program" will always hit me with a big punch of hurt. Why? It meant to me their wrongful assessment and failure to see what was really producing my behaviours. It seems almost obscene that they could not. *"How can you not see it? Are you blind? Stupid?"* And all it did was make my anger escalate. They isolated me from the rest of the class, shoved me in the back of the classroom and told me to "keep quiet" while they "teach the other children." I tried to look insolent, like a rebel who didn't care. I was churning inside. There were some teachers then who only made things worse. My grade-eight year was met with a tall slim woman, near retirement, who had a very low tolerance for what she perceived as disobedience. So, when we were introduced to one another, it went south very fast. Right from the first day my skinny early-teen body walked through her classroom door it was war. I think she thought I would somehow bend to her will and that my bad-ass self would soon be whipped into shape. "Don't think you're going to get away with anything – not while you're under my thumb." Under. Yup, deep south. By that time, I may not have been able to crawl back up even if I'd wanted to.

She obviously didn't know that, the entire time I was at odds with her, it wasn't being done purposefully. Under the hood I was a kind and compassionate young man, or so I thought. "All I want is for you to treat me like the rest of the kids!" I wanted to scream. But this dark force that was left undetected for so long, had command of, not only my heart and mind, but also over any abilities to perform academically. I couldn't fulfill what I was there for, and she couldn't reach it. It was a dark kind of standoff, with no comprehension on either side.

Forced into a program I knew wasn't for me, it served only to take my darkness and turn it ink-black. There was clearly more going on inside of me than met their eye, yet I was powerless to tell them. The lower form of education and the assumption that I was stupid? "I have no control, no control I can show!" I'd whisper to myself, hyper-ventilating. If a heart could be felt to break, that's what I felt." Yeah, I know you've washed your hands of me!" I'd sputter. I felt my stomach twisting, my breath caught, my hands shaking. Their decision to give up on me reinforced the again-and-again feeling of abandonment. Just a kid, trying to figure it all out on my own.

There I was, off in a back corner staring at a three-ringed binder and trying to nurse a completely broken spirit. "I must be stupid," I began thinking. "That's how they all see me to be, stupid and someone who can't make anything of themselves. They're adults and know more." As time went on, I began to see the separation from my classmates materialize. I began to understand that my violent and vocal pleas for help had placed me in a box. If there had been disconnect before, that I was already struggling to come to terms with, this made it much bigger. It just grew, like some science-fiction blob. Next to it, my young preteen self kept shrinking, and totally solo..

Imagine what it feels like to be placed on the outside by your classmates. Many of us have been there, but to be isolated by the teachers too? I went to school day after day and was told "Just sit there, I don't have time for you." This kind of statement often was followed up by the ever-popular line "Go to the office." It was like a broken record, and they kept spinning it. Soon, it got so that I didn't have to lose my temper. *They* reacted to what they thought would come next. "Can't blame you for that," I say now. "But if you'd only even acted like it mattered, like I mattered. maybe we wouldn't have had all those stand-offs."

In their eyes, like those of my fourth-grade teacher, I was a write-off. As a result, whatever was wreaking havoc inside my head just became one with me, before I graduated from the coldest place I had ever known. But only two years before my departure, it was during that time they were doing their damnedest to ship me, dumb me off, "offload their problem" on to another school.

"That would have been okay," I'd say to myself. "But it was a school for the intellectually-impaired. I would not have fit in there. Mom and Dad – you knew it, and so did I." This is what assumption can do to your life.

But I had a very strong-willed mother advocating for me and who prevented the move. That prevented my union with my depressive-like symptoms from being a total disaster.

So, What is the Damage?

When I stop to evaluate my years at this school, all I can think about is how wrong they got it. They just didn't know and didn't have the time or desire to explore it. My entire young life was defined by the observations of people who I needed to help me. Instead, they shoved me in a corner, labeled me a slow learner and gave me the distinction of the school's problem child. This may not have been their goal but solving behavioral-related issues just wasn't on the radar in those days. And yet the damage was done. Its reverberation has been a kind of lifelong companion I don't want but maybe don't know how to live without. It's just part of me.

The biggest lesson I learned from my years in school was that I wasn't worth the time or the effort. I was useless. This feeling echoed in my head, like when yelling in the vast country. The sentence, "You'll never amount to anything!" was like this awful anthem over everything else.

Because of my parents, I left my junior-high school on my terms. For all those years, I was hardly ever granted the power to choose – but now I had it. So, when the day came when we officially graduated, I walked up to the principal – who I have no memory of – and accepted my diploma. After the handshake and the "Good luck next year," I walked past him and ripped the neatly-rolled piece of paper in half. I can still remember the sound that thick paper made as it tore.

CHAPTER THREE

Hitting High School and Experiencing Sad Realities

"As if growing up and never feeling a sense of belonging wasn't bad enough...during times of loss I couldn't even grieve as a kid because the adults leaned on me for support."

By the time I turned fifteen, a time when there are lots of hormones at work, the physical outbursts were pretty much non-existent. This reduction in my temper must have had to do with the gentle approach of my first therapist, and moving on to high school. This large brick structure made my previous school look like a tree-fort in comparison. Built sometime when my mother was young, the school had this pale-yellow carpet, dated orange lockers, and wood paneling and cinder block everywhere you looked.

My fists had a much-needed break, but I began to find myself more and more worried inside about many things. These things seemed irrational, and difficult to get to. It was a replacement to that internal, all-consuming mental pain, but it was nothing good.

Maybe it's because I didn't know what to call this internal discomfort. Or maybe all I knew was anger, so I was just that – angry. It wasn't till I was an adult that I could say to myself: "Ah – this feeling of constant worry is probably generalized anxiety disorder!"

New Friendship

There were some experiences that tagged along with me from my old school to the new, in the "general" education path. Just like in my junior high, it produced the feeling of loneliness and isolation, a feeling of being a sort of second-class citizen. There was a difference, though. My new educational setting was so large that I hardly ever ran into one of my old schoolmates. That was a relief in the initial days and weeks, but I felt more alone than I had ever felt to date. Good and bad, up and down. One thing the enormity of my high school gave me was to allow me to work off a blank slate.

And, just like at my hometown school, I had few friends. By the time I landed in my new homeroom on that first day, I felt that I wasn't worthy enough to have anyone want to be my friend, so I kept to myself. "Best that way," I'd tell myself. "Don't even try. It doesn't work." I knew I was talking more to myself, but I guess myself was "company." As well, my confidence for academics also took a beating. I didn't seem able to absorb what I needed to do, produced jumbled results, and even handed in blank papers.

As the year went along, there was this persistent feeling that I didn't belong, and not only on a peer-to-peer level. I felt like I wasn't supposed to be in this watered-down version of an education program.

Although I would eventually hang around with a few people, there was one boy I was really drawn to. A tall pale kid with a love for comics, music and video games, he often wore a black trench coat that matched not only his hair but also the black boots he wore everywhere he went.

We had so many things in common, and just never got tired of being together. Like me, he seemed to have some inner demons that hijacked a lot of his happiness. And yet we were happy together. "Misery loves company, I guess," I would tell myself.

In a sea of testosterone and at an age where every little ordeal was a mountain of pain, we kept each other sane enough to not only get through the standard teenage stuff but to keep this unseen force at bay. Looking back on our friendship, I can now fully appreciate just how much we, two gangly and reclusive teens, needed one another if we were to survive the inner turmoil that raged in both of us. Some of my best memories of this time were of him and me walking miles and miles to get anywhere. Some days we skipped school and headed to his grandfather's place.

It was an escape from our school of pain, and this old man was generally happy to see us, though he asked a few times "Why are you out of school?"

"Oh, professional development day." "Oh – a day off for everyone, while they fix the heating system."

Other days were spent chowing down on junk food. Or, as we called it, "grindage," code for chips, pop and chocolate. We were like bottomless pits, eating away while playing the original PlayStation game.

It was the best of the '90s (or the worst, our parents might have thought). And whether the music was on the Hot Charts or not, it really spoke to us. Just what was it about rap we loved? That strength in repetitiveness, the messages that were brazen, shouted out and even obscene. Later we'd find out it was called the most important event shaping the musical structural of the American charts. All we knew then was that it spoke to us.

All the Smoke, Dreams and Nightmares, Why Would I Stop, Murder Rap and Funhouse, Public Enemy, N.W.A., Ice-T and Ice Cube – we loved it all, and loved the partying as well. There was booze flowing, drugs passed around, gangsta bravado...but I mostly remember the energy of the music. And I know many people don't think of it as "music," just loud repetitive noise. But it flowed through our blood, and we went through so much of it together. It's the kind of thing that made us really close, because it defined our lives.

Although we have taken long sabbaticals away from each other's company, the friendship remains intact and strong and I think it always will be.

You Can't Do That

"I'm much more capable than this situation dictates!" I would say to myself. Well, I might have known this, but being automatically enrolled in the general program left my new teachers with the assumption I was there because I had learning difficulties. "Why would you think any other way?" I say to "them" now.

Despite knowing I was working well below my capabilities, I went on and did what I could in high school. Paid attention, tried to apply myself to my lessons, lugged homework home. I kept out of trouble for the most part, landing myself in the office only when I defended myself or someone else against the isolated bully. "Sir (or Ma'am), this is wrong. This person did not start the fight. *That* person did." It seems I developed an affinity for helping the underdog. Other than that, my years in high school were unremarkable and probably typical except I was far less social. I would sometimes go to dances and parties, and a hangout up town late into the night.

With the exception of a few outbursts, I did my best to complete my assignments with care and attention. I hated being in the class for "slow learner." I buckled down because my classmates were not my people and they knew it. I can remember a slim young lady with a big attitude. Every time she walked by my desk, she would knock my belongings to the floor or mutter "Asshole" and other obscenities under her breath as she sauntered from her seat and back again. Something began to bubble under my surface.

"Asshole."

One day, I exploded at her and said something to the effect of "I may look like an easy target but I am far from it! Just keep it up and see."

I was so intense, like a wolf growling over its dinner, that she took a step back and looked afraid, no words sputtering out of her mouth. She never bothered me again. While I felt bad afterwards, my outburst immersed me in a shield of protection from the onlookers who were also having a go at me. From that day forward, I never had another issue with anyone.

Truthfully, all I wanted to do was get to the end of a decades-long battle with a system that had successfully done more harm than good. It had left me with a whole new set of language that I call negative self-script. "John, all the adults telling you that you can't do the work of the other children, must be true. Otherwise, why would they tell you such things?"

"I am too stupid," I'd think. Even now, when I mess up I sometimes yell, "Jesus, you're stupid."

As a result, a slow sadness burned away and dulled down the greatest moments of my life. Over the years, I could feel that "Depression, you were almost certainly made worse by the very adults who were supposed to help me." It would get that foothold and never let up on it. Sometimes, it's a mere ache, lying at the bottom of my heart. Other times it's so intense, it leaves me bedridden.

I was made to feel as though I would never amount to anything meaningful. It was the way I'd have tools yanked out of my hands when my father saw me struggle, or a math teacher who made my life hell just for asking a question. I can recall being in her class one day, raising my hand for help. "This stuff is hard to understand."

Her response? "Not right now. I don't have time for you people." Her phrase "You people" was immediately cemented into my head. Oh, I was one of the "You People" No more John Arenburg, individual human being. And that voice and what it said – and in spite of being a bit weathered by the passage of time – still serves as a roadblock to any progress I make.

Even with all of my ordeals, there has always been something deep inside of me that knew differently. Knowing this in my heart gave me the necessary courage to somehow "show them all." Just before graduating high school with top marks in English and history, I had decided to find a profession helping others. This had always been clear to me – that I had a knack for it, so why not make a living at something I figured I'd be good at?

After some reflection, I decided that becoming a paramedic would satisfy my insatiable desire to help others. What better way to help people who were in their darkest hours, their times of great pain, accidents and near-death?

Something profound happened to me when I had made that fateful decision. It gave me some sense of control, which

I can hardly recall ever having. It was a sort-of light-bulb moment when, for the first time in my life, a sense of inner calm washed over me, and it seemed to grow from somewhere deep within. It was though I had woken my purpose, finally. Was this normality? "Is this what it's like to be like the other kids?" I would ask myself. Man, I felt good. I felt what I could only describe as joy, and it kept going on.

Like a practitioner of meditation, I realized I had ended up getting in touch with my long-buried "authentic" self, the person who wanted to do some good. Looking back through my childhood, I realized that there was a long list of helping others – from holding doors at the age of four, to helping a classmate talk about his sexual assault while we worked on an assignment in an empty classroom, to raising money for UNICEF in grade seven.

But it was in my teen years that I really began to shine. Other kids would confidently tell me about their problems, and I would listen. I even helped someone through the pain of a suicide attempt at fifteen. When I decided that the emergency services were the perfect career choice for me, it came after this revelation of my long history of helping others. "Being a helper is my authentic self," I concluded. Suddenly, it all made sense. Finally, I was freed from the clutches of all the teachers who told me I couldn't do this, and I couldn't do that. For the first time in my life, I had made a decision that was truly my own.

This feeling of Zen, a peaceful, warm feeling of calm, turned out to be a flash in the frying pan when I decided to approach the high-school guidance counsellor about my career choice. Full of nervous excitement, my chest heavy and a tongue tied in knots, I allowed this newly-found feeling that I had finally taken control of my life, to overpower the angst of sitting down with the counsellor to make a life-changing decision.

I remember sitting across from this thin-haired man with a quick smile and booming voice that I always felt didn't suit him, and explaining to him that I wanted to go to school to become a paramedic. I don't recall the conversation word-for-word, but I can recall his response to my post-secondary choice. Looking over his glasses, he said, "You can't do that. You need grade twelve academic."

When that one short sentence rolled off his tongue and his deep voice seemed to pound my ears, I felt what I thought was my authentic self, instantly buried alive in what felt like an avalanche of pain. What remained of any strip of confidence I'd had was verbally shot dead, just like that.

All at once, the little boy in me was revived, as all those familiar feelings of defeat and sadness came rushing back. There was a difference this time, though, from my traditional reaction. My spirit was crushed, and any prospect of regaining it impossible.

Outside of School

In my adolescence I spent spending hours and hours up in my bedroom. It was a large room with sky-blue walls and a slanted ceiling that my head had made forceful contact with on more than one occasion. The mess contained within the four walls was like that of any typical teen, a path to the bed and dishes that were there so long they were growing their own ecosystem.

It was here I spent most of my time, sitting in silence just writing poems and song lyrics, trying to understand the demons that kept knocking on my door. I also listened to music constantly. A lot. It was a tool to help regulate my highs and lows. It was my saving grace through those turbulent and troubling times. I'm sure the neighbors didn't enjoy my loud version of therapy, but I had to cling to it. "Deep depressive state...go away, stay away, let the music kill you."

Like most teens full of raw emotion produced by a host of chemical changes, I dated and had a few girlfriends, but I found that the slip into darker spaces, together with this sensitivity that seemed a part of me, did more to fracture my relationships than bond them. Lost and confused about where my sadness was coming from, I often grew irritated and short, leaving those I dated feeling a bit put off by the sudden and frequent changes in mood. I remember being so upset and frustrated with myself when I had a moment of emotional upheaval. I was hard on myself because it was usually not intentional. I often would say to myself "What the hell is wrong with you? You're always messing things up."

When the relationship inevitably came to an end, I was devastated nearly every time. It can't be unusual for teens to have their hearts broken, but for me its intensity held on in ways that seemed to drag out the deep sense of dread I so often felt in those days.

Tragedy Strikes

The agonizing worry I had (earlier) intensified with the first death of a very close family member, my grandfather. A short man with a quick wit and thick-lensed glasses, he had worked hard since the age of fourteen. I know this had made him dream of a different life for himself. And for me, because I went the first six years without a father figure, he played the role of both grandfather and father. For me, the sun rose and set on this man, the moon too. To this day, I can still hear him ask me, "Do you want a snort of 7Up?" Of course, I always said yes. He would go to the cupboard and get his shot glass that he kept on a high shelf, fill it full of the fizzy clear pop and say, "There you go, boy."

It was a devastating blow for me when he died. My first-ever experience with death and it was a doozy. Despite the fact that I was trying to deal with my own grief, I recall being a rock of comfort-strength for everyone around me, the day of the funeral. I sat there with one aunt on one side of me and a second aunt on the other. Both were crying so I did my best to help them get through one of the most difficult days of their lives by holding their hands. I remember shortly after the funeral, hearing one of my aunts tell another, "Boy, John was so much help, like a rock he was. How would we have managed without him? He's becoming a man." Little did they know, a part of me died that day.

Although it was many years ago, I don't remember shedding a single tear. I guess I went into a "helper" mode. It's always been an integral part of who I am. It's as though I was pre-programmed to help others, but in this scenario, my own bereavement be damned. This quality inside me seemed to push down on my ability to grieve as I should have been allowed to do.

And I would tell myself, "Helping my family through the loss was a perfectly good place to put my own grief." By helping others get through it, I was able to place it on the back shelf and for years, on the back shelf it remained. But although I tried to avoid it, my body refused to. I became numb and like an angel watching from above. I felt like a passive observer in someone else's tragedy. But it was my own.

Looking back now, I feel like the flames of my generalized anxiety disorder were first ignited at this point in my life. I had just suffered the loss of one of the most important people in my life. I became a worst-case scenario thinker, worrying about everything and obsessing over thoughts of losing those I loved. Just a mere passing thought of losing a loved one produced enough fear to send me into a panic attack.

In a matter of only weeks after Granddad's funeral, I walked the earth with a sense of dread and fear. It was a heavy weight that sat on my chest, only I didn't seem to feel this discomfort from the inside, but rather, it was a heavy thing that lay just below the surface. I stayed up many nights writing more than I had ever before. I would sit at a homemade desk my father had built for me, squinting in the dim light produced by a tiny lamp, hoping it would help lift the burden produced by a "who's next?" type of mindset. I began to write more and more – more suddenly, more fully, more unable to stop.

Being in my adolescence and experiencing my first-ever tragedy, I was not ready, with the means to deal with death and loss and what it had awoken in me. I honestly felt at the time that "I've dealt with you, grief. That's it." In reality I never once looked back to see if there were any residual bits of pain deep within. How could I look for them? I had no idea how.

And as many of us know, the teenage years are turbulent at the best of times. How do you reach through that to uncover the source of emotional distress? I can ask myself, as a therapist might, "Is my inner turmoil a function of regular development for me, or is there some underlying, more serious condition that needs attention?" What role did the sensitive young boy play in all this – and what I am today?

Regardless, I was lost in the standard tagline, that of being told by the adults in my life that teenagers are "moody," "filled with ups and downs due to hormonal fluctuations." Despite what I was being told, it ate away at me. This couldn't be normal, could it? I can recall feeling something wasn't as it should be because of it. I became obsessively fascinated with the human condition, sitting down and writing out my own theories on why people grieve and what causes them to go through bouts of anger. I didn't want only to know the answer – I needed one.

I would later come to the conclusion that two things happened when my life intersected with the loss of my grandfather. One, I would come to turn every thought into chaos and as a result, fear the world – and two, I never fully recovered from the loss. I suspect that an undiagnosed depression would take hold of me and settle in for the long haul.

In my youth, I had mistaken the act of shoving my personal tragedies such as the death of my grandfather deep down in my guts. In my limited life's experience, I thought this was an effective way of dealing with all the mental pain. I didn't intentionally tell myself to "bottle it up!" as I had no skills to do that. Cognitive skills, as the experts say. I simply had to move on and survive. Despite this, I understood that keeping my emotions in and holding back was not a cure. But after Granddad's death, there were several other deaths in the family, a series, you might say. Every time one occurred, I was denied another chance to mourn. It meant, as I found out, that I remained "emotionally immature" in this area.

As I look back, I would give anything to have this moment of my grandfather's passing, back. I should have been the one propped up by the adults, not the other way around. "Where is my chance to grieve?" I would ask myself. I may have been young at the time, but I knew I needed a sturdy wall from my elders to lean on. "What about me?" Damn. I was just a kid!

Even after the dust settled, no one in my family ever came to my aid, ever checked in to see if I was okay. That still cuts deep to this day. "Once again, I'm let down by the grownups in my life," I often thought. It ignited a combination of anger and hopelessness within me. Even now, this mixed emotional feeling echoes in my head.

Today, looking back, I would say "Now, I am curious to know if this increased my odds of becoming post-traumatic today. One thing I am certain of, it was what fostered the growth of my depression."

CHAPTER FOUR

The Road Toward Mental Illness

"Do I regret the day I signed up to be a firefighter? I'm afraid the answer is yes. Would I do it all over again? Absolutely."

My final year came to its end – and I was back in my familiar world of isolation and despair. However, there was still that spark, dancing inside me. "I am not going to give up on a future that's mine for the taking." In an act of appropriate defiance, I would enroll for an academic upgrade and try for what *I* wanted – and not allow others to distract me from my goals and rob me of my passion.

During my high school years, between grade eleven and graduation, I thought a lot about paramedicine, what it would be like to save lives. I could envision myself rushing to the rig, jumping on board and being "the guy" that saved someone's life. I thought, "Wouldn't it be wonderful if I could do this every day?" My daydreaming about saving people would continuously reaffirm that this was what I wanted to do. "I know I've been made to feel like I won't succeed but I know I can do this. I am going to realize this dream."

All I wanted was to be the one who makes a real difference in the lives of people at their most vulnerable. Composed and healed – well, nearly healed – from the "You can't do this" phrase that came from the mouth of my guidance counsellor, I remember asking myself; "What do I have to do to get there?"

Go for an academic upgrade. Of course, this was just one piece of the puzzle. But even so, it was enough to tell myself,

"I'm tired of people telling me that I can't do it, and I will prove them all wrong."

Grade twelve academic upgrade year was an experience of the same old, same old, teachers telling me "It's tough! Challenging. And it will be a struggle for you." One teacher actually suggested, "Maybe you don't belong here" I can vividly recall the vice-principal saying to me, "You should have gone to the adult school. This is no place for you!"

I remember thinking that his strong reaction to my re-enrollment was unjustified. "Just chill, dude!" So, I said a few colourful words under my breath to the naysayers, and just kept moving forward. Undeterred by their comments, I managed to get through the year in academic, proving to them that I was at least more capable than I was ever credited for. "Take that!" I said to myself when I received my diploma by mail. "Nah, I'm not going to sit in that hot, overcrowded arena again, been there done that." Not only did I prove to them that I was capable – I also proved it to my biggest naysayer, myself.

Between this revelation and later on, my experience as a firefighter, I realized that I was focused on being a paramedic. I could take this "Do what you have to" approach and apply it to every challenge life threw at me.

From the moment this revelation clicked and helped me punch holes in the walls of fear, I adopted it as my guide. This has served me well throughout my life, and I credit it with why I am still here today. It has always been the pillar of not only my success, but also of my survival.

From a Boy to a Man?

As fate would have it, a relative who was in the local volunteer fire department would show up on the doorstep with an application for "junior firefighter" in hand. He was a cousin of mine, a much older man with a fun-loving nature. He reminded me a bit of Santa Claus, and all that was missing was the beard.

I remember standing in my parents' small, well-lit kitchen trying to take in what was being offered. "Firefighter? I'd be a *firefighter?*" I found out later that a "junior" is a clever way to try to recruit future firefighters by signing up under-aged individuals to participate in training, training like that of regular members but without any real on-scene stuff.

Although I felt trepidation at the offer, sure enough the helper inside of me pushed forward. And when I realized that this could be a huge benefit to my paramedic goals, any reservations I was feeling melted away like ice on an early spring day. With my parents' blessing, I accepted the application and turned it in the next week. Little did I realize that this one decision would steer me down the road to mental illness, a narrow road that would force a face-to-face meeting with PTSD.

It wasn't long after, that I received a call to come down to the station for an interview. This was a minor formality because they were anxious to get the program going. One week later I was standing in the cold truck bay packed with bright-red fire trucks and a dozen grown men I had nothing in common with. I was nervous, but I was excited. Few words were exchanged, I was met with a few half-hearted hellos, and the rest of the time I stood in awkward silence while they returned to their conversation.

Not long after I arrived in the station, I was ushered upstairs by unseen voices from the back of the station. All I heard was "Are any of the yup here yet?" This was followed by one of the firefighters saying, "You here to be a junior?"

I responded with a grainy "yes."

His response was abrupt. "Go to the back and go through the door on the right." I followed his instructions and found myself in a small, totally-white stairwell. Because the man's directions ended at "Take the door at the right," I understood that going up the stairs was the only option I had.

In the end, there were four of us juniors and the instructor. My excitement was dashed somewhat when he informed us, "Okay – the majority of your time is going to be textbook learning for the first few months. You need the theory."

Our instructor, a skinny man with a moustache, and a tendency to never stop moving, ended up being one of the most skilled firefighters I would ever serve with. I don't think I ever saw him without his trusty travel mug of tea in his hand, even on the training ground. He was a strong-willed and passionate man, who loved the service. I can still hear him say, "If the day comes when you think you have learned all there is to know about the fire service, that's the day you need to get out because you're going to kill someone with that attitude."

He was very thorough and had a way of making the mundane material easy to grasp. Despite this, all the uncertainty and fear around whether I could be a firefighter or not, swirled around in my head. Before I even sat down and opened the firefighter training manual, I convinced myself that "John, you'll never be confident enough to be a real, productive, contributing member of this team."

Choosing to join the fire department was the most monumental, life-changing decision I have ever made. Its cold hard reality ripped me out of childhood and thrust me into the world of adult reality. I learned structure and how to respect a hierarchical order, both of which I needed in those latter years of adolescence. I took school more seriously, and by the time I went back to upgrade for an academic diploma, I understood the importance of that document.

Perhaps the most fundamentally important lesson I have learned being a firefighter was that no matter what it was I feared, I had to put that aside and do whatever it takes to make things right.

Between these revelations and my later experience as a firefighter, I realized that I could take this "Do what you have to" approach and apply it to every challenge life threw at me. This would later include my long battle with mental illness.

When you're crouched at a doorway with dark grey smoke billowing from underneath the door, sirens screaming off in the distance and your commanding officer hollering at you to "Get going!" there's no turning back. And there's no one to take your place. The task of extinguishing the fire was yours and your partner's, no backing out. Someone had to run into the flames' stinging, roaring heat and orange glow to minimize its chaos. On some runs, I was that guy at the door. Before entering, an officer would say something like; "Once there's a crew in place to back you up, then you can make entry." Or "The fire is on the second floor, west side."

It wasn't long before I learned that this "must do" approach had real value way beyond the fire ground. As juniors we had it drilled into our heads that "We do what we must to help our community. Putting yourselves in harm's way is the job you signed up for." A notion that became a reality for me when I turned nineteen and became a full-fledged active member of the department. You may think "reality" is going into the service, being a hero and saving lives. Tragedy's actual reality has zero similarities. When it plays out in front of you in real time, you are ill-prepared to deal with its outcome. It either changes you slowly over time or devastates you instantly. Regardless of who you are, it changes you in some way.

One of its harshest lessons is the fact that you can't save everyone, a reality that is so difficult to come to grips with. As I learned, you can't own what you can't control. It will slowly sicken your soul and tear you in two.

For me, transitioning from a junior to a bona fide firefighter was the moment I turned directly on the road to mental illness. I just didn't know it. Turns out, it would take years to realize that I had never let my first "fatal call" go. The sight, the smell, and the contrast of the cool September air of that evening is forever seared into my memory. Like a permanent scar that never faded, it torments me to this day.

On this fall evening, we were dispatched to a structure fire, an eight-by-ten barn on fire. Being young and new to the active side of the service, I jumped to my feet and ran for the fire hall which was only a few hundred meters away from where I was sitting. When adrenaline takes over, you don't think, you just do.

That adrenaline rush was carried over when we initially arrived on the scene. So, when the news came that there was someone inside, I really didn't think about it until the fire was extinguished and things had calmed down.

I recall vividly, a veteran firefighter and I were heading through a field that was directly behind the scene to cut off traffic on the adjacent road, so as to keep the scene as secure as possible. During our walk, I asked him, "Is what I'm smelling – *him*?"

He said, "Yes, that's the smell of burnt flesh, and it's a smell that you will never forget."

It was in that very moment that I regretted asking the question because my mind was slammed into "park," and any thoughts I had, became jumbled. It was as though someone had electrocuted my brain from the inside. I also recall him speaking of his own first experience of someone who died in this way, or at least that's what I thought he was telling me. His words were muffled and made no sense to me because I felt like I was a million miles away. This, despite being a foot apart. Fairly sure that's when my mind went into "safe mode." Like any piece of machinery, it was being protected – and for me, from the trauma of one of the hardest days of my adult life.

When I arrived home, around 3:00 a.m., I felt terror race through me. It was terror of the person who had passed in such an unbelievable manner. *He's coming to get me*. Every time I closed my eyes the sights, smells and sounds prompted me back awake. I kept asking myself, "Am I going crazy?" I've never been more terrified in my entire life then I was in those early morning hours.

Think I would have quit then? It would be enough of a reason. But I would end up devoting fifteen years of my life to the fire service and as the years went by, the accumulation of the chaos took me apart at the seams and took up residence in my soul. Over the years, it rebuilt my mind. It would debilitate me to the point where my life's course would be forever altered.

Although far from the only endeavour in my life that had such a door-slamming impact on me, it is the "core" of the long bone of my mental demise. There are moments where I absolutely hated making that fateful decision, to walk through the bay doors all those years ago. I was just a kid and too sensitive to fend off the aftermath of death and the other horrors that come with serving in the service. Many emergencies later, I am haunted by most of the deaths and dismemberments I have witnessed.

It got to the point where every call I went to where the results were tragic, I would automatically be thrust into autopilot in an attempt to save my mind from being consumed by the accumulation of losses. I can remember with regularity the same words bouncing around in my head every time I was on or near the darker calls. In my head I would be shouting "I can't do this, I can't take much more, something has to give. After this call I'm finished!"

But that didn't happen right away. Back in those days, the pressure was enormous to ignore it, and to push it deep down. So, like in the days following my grandfather's funeral, and in the years that followed, I pushed it way down deep, manned up and found myself jumping on the back of a fire truck and heading out to the next call. I countered the panic in my head by saying things like "The next time you won't feel this need to shut down, and maybe you just found the last death call harder than you should have...?"

In my later years in the service, I began to associate everything Fire Department-related with trauma. The numbness, the disassociation. The level-ten anxiety, lit up every time the sirens would wail.

The Evolution of a Philosophical Doctrine

As far back as I can recall, this blond-headed little boy that I had long grown out of physically, was still the predominant figure inside when it came to trying new things. I was frightened to death at the prospect of trying something new, going to college, taking a course at firefighter school, you name it. The fear lingers to this day. In some moments, it rages in me as real and as intense as any call I'd ever been on. Other times, it is hanging in the middle of my dramatic scale, always on, always present and unrelenting.

Looking back, I often wondered how I had it in me to manhandle the waves of courage to deal with the worst death had to offer. I guess my desire to help others gave me the needed strength to beat back the fear and lack of confidence. "All I want to do is help, and I think being a firefighter can be how I can do the best." I remember thinking that joining the Volunteer Fire Department would be a great way to find out if I could actually do the job of a paramedic. Both emergency services overlapped in a lot of ways and besides, the fire-service training was free, and good on a resume.

Once I had some experience, accumulated by putting myself in harm's way, I recall thinking after a tragic call was behind me, "I can't believe I was strong enough to do what had to be done on that call." Given that I had a hesitancy beaten into me by the words "You can't do that" for nearly all my life – there I was, defying that narrative and I was doing it well! I created other narratives: "Wow! I can do this, I'm not as stupid as I thought I was, and I will succeed and I will show them all." And, "Hey, if I had the courage to go beyond the door of a house fire, what else am I capable of?"

Thanks, Mom

Around the same time, I was learning to take on the world as a young man and at the same time, put distance between me and that chronic feeling of being a failure. But beyond the experiences of childhood, I had to own my part in the journey I was on. But more than that, I had to take charge of my life and make something out of this gift I've been given.

I was with my mother one day when I was mad at the world for thrusting me into adulthood ill-prepared to succeed. I turned to her, feeling the anger throbbing in me. I think I said quite a lot in the beginning, but mostly remember saying "This system has severely stunted my development."

We sat across from one another in the front room of her home, a room split evenly into one-part living room and the other half dining room. She listened to me go on saying things like, "It's the school's fault for where I am! If only this had been different, if only they had listened to me, I'd be much better off today."

Her deep blue eyes were opened wide and riveted on me. Moving her fingers through her curly black hair, she said, "Son, you can spend the rest of your life blaming others for your problems, but you're nineteen now and are old enough to take responsibility for your own actions, for what you do with your life moving forward, regardless of who did you wrong in the past." Her tone, gentle as it was, made me sit up and listen.

Her words gripped me.. It was almost magical. They rang so loudly with their truth that I immediately knew I could start to craft my experiences of my youth with a fresh perspective. You would expect a revelation like that to come more slowly, but it really was like that. Maybe it had been working away inside me, and just needed to be set free.

Yes, my history did set me off course, but my mother's words had just illustrated this: that in reality, I was and always have been the pilot who controls the direction my life takes, and therefore I had the power to control the direction I ventured in. Ever since that day, I have lived by a saying, "You have a choice where to put your energy." So, when things seem insurmountable, I make a conscious decision to put my mental energy into my recovery.

When I replay this period of my life in my head, I now realize that I was constantly panicked inside, a feeling that came out of my life's journey, the years of feeling like I would never amount to anything, and the decade and a half my mental health was assaulted by responding to car accidents, house fires and heart attacks. But at the time, I was pinning and slapping all my woes on my youth. This ended up being just a piece of the puzzle that had me turned upside down.

The chaos that brought about my first casualty as a firefighter had blown up this self-blame and panic and lit the fuse that would eventually lead to my near-total mental demise. I was angry, constantly stressed and feeling how years in the fire service had taken their toll. And I had lost my marriage.

I was really struggling with it and feeling hopeless in its wake at the time my mother and I had this monumental chat. There has never been another moment in my life where words were so potent and made such an impact. Despite my having seen things one should never see, her words propelled me forward. I could feel myself letting go of the blame.

Picture a wardrobe of old clothes that could keep you imprisoned but should be discarded. Once free of that, I could feel myself beginning to accept my part in my life's course. Being hit by this revelation was like being liberated from jail. I was able to let go of the past and do what I had to do, on the way to making a life for myself. It would take a few years, but I finally took the reins of my future and applied for college, a moment and action that would change my life forever.

So, I combined the teachings of the fire service – mainly the one that taught me that you have to "do it" regardless of how you feel – with the wise words from the mouth of my mother. Out of that fusion I would find I was able to overcome adversity and follow the path expected of any young person. Go to school, get a job, and settle down.

But it did more than that for me. It also helped me to push back against the persistent sadness and anxiety that had been so dominating during my youth. The entire time I worked to establish my life as a young man, I would live relatively free from my mental pain. "Finally, finally...you are living!" I said to myself.

CHAPTER FIVE

Moving Towards Normalcy

"Happiness, it has an ebb and flow to it. Like the universe, it's not a constant. So, if I had known that pain and suffering were part of the deal, I can't help but wonder if things would be different today...?"

College! By the time I applied for and was accepted, I had seen enough death and destruction play out in front of me that any desire I had to become a paramedic was gone. It was like it had been rotted, corrupted by a small but mighty accumulation of a numbing feeling of dread.

Where did this dread come from? It was born out of an illusion built like some demented ancient ziggurat temple – with lots of components – of preconceived notions. Notions such as ideas of what the fire service was like, versus its cold and unforgiving reality. As you bear witness to something so out of the norm like an unnatural death, I found, you really struggle to make sense of what you are seeing.

I decided that "helping people with their mental wellbeing would be best" – as it would be the polar opposite of helping to fight physical injury and loss of life.

What I have to do, I thought, is enroll in something that still feeds my desire to help, but is more on the psychological end of the spectrum.

My partner at the time was in college, a college that I knew had a variety of programs. Shortly after making the decision to change my life's course, I summoned up enough courage to ask her "Can you look and see if the Human Services program is offered at your campus? I thank this may be the direction I want to take, career-wise."

As I recall, she happily agreed to find out for me. And within days, she and I were staring down at the course requirements and description. As I read the description, I got more and more excited. I said to myself, "This sounds like something I'd love to do." So, I excitedly filled out the application for both the course and the necessary paperwork for the student loan I would need if I were accepted.

Then the opening came – I was accepted into the Human Services program, a course designed to provide students with a general understanding of many different "helping fields," and an intro to long-term care work, mostly. Its other function was to prepare you for a second year if you chose to take it. Second year was a specialization.

Finally, My Time Had Come

Getting accepted into community college felt like both a huge accomplishment and a big relief. After all, I'd spent my entire life being told I couldn't do this, couldn't do that, and had some long-lasting, destructive effects. I know that if I hadn't adopted the philosophy of "just get it done regardless of your level of fear," I would never have graced the community college's doorstep. Turns out that that pressure to perform was just what I needed. I recall having a second wave of empowerment, like that of the one I had in high school when I had decided to become a paramedic.

While I was obviously nervous about the new adventure I was about to embark on, I can recall feeling like I did when I first learned to swim in the deep end of a pool. I envisioned myself on the diving board, working up the nerve to jump. After what seemed like an hour of fighting with myself, I finally said "The heck with it." And jumped in. Like that hot summer day at the pool, I ran through my fear of going to school again and dove right into it. "The heck with it" I heard echo in my head.

Having worked up the courage to throw myself down the road of life, I was met at the door with the well-conditioned phrases that had dominated me my entire life: "I can't do this." "It's not for me." "I'm going to fail." "You're going to fail." From somewhere I found the strength to manhandle them out of the way, walk into the lobby of that college and turn the crank of a new adventure.

The inside of this higher-learning institution did not coincide with the vision I had in my head for what a college should look like. I was disappointed by its appearance. As I looked around, I felt my high school. Except for the wood panelling, the environment was made up of long hallways, walls that were made of painted white cinder blocks, just like that of the school I had graduated from a few years before. I also felt my gut pummelled with recognition to see that drab and familiar format, with lockers on one side and classrooms cut into the walls on the other.

Same sense of familiarity with the classrooms: chalkboard up front, windows running down on one side and a standard desk, designated for the instructor. The only real difference was that instead of desks, there were tables for the students to gather around. Walking through the door of my assigned class, I felt, all over again, the environment of my grade-four classroom. Any sense of excitement I may have had was further deflated like air out of a balloon. But I knew I had to set the resurgence of feelings brought on by this similar environment. I told myself, "This is college, this is more likely than not to be an entirely different experience."

Although I had spent a few years out of school, I had no reference that helped me ease into this college life. The building itself may have been a carbon copy of my high school, but the academic learning environment was not.

One of the side effects of my educational experience up to this point in my life was that of survival. With that, came improvisation. In public school I learned the art of negotiation through my daily controversy, especially in middle school. I honed this skill because I was always trying to reduce my punishments.

I once called my junior-high teacher a "bitch" because I was so tired of her treating me like I was nothing. So, as was the norm, I was sent to the office, and I remember as well just trying to get someone, anyone, to understand my plight. I recall saying to the principal, "I feel really bad for calling her that because it's the one swear word I hate." Of course, I didn't feel that way, I was simply trying to lighten the severity of my punishment. I hated doing this, but the teachers and principal had all the power. I was but a child, and needed to find a way of defending my actions. While on the surface calling her a bitch dictated a consequence, that's exactly what she was. It was in those formative years that I slowly started to learn to advocate for myself. "Her behaviour just isn't right." I often said to myself. "Why is she allowed to be so mean and nasty but I'm the one who gets in trouble for defending myself? I hate injustice!"

I also learned how to cut corners academically, often making up oral assignments on the spot. "I'll just read a bit of the beginning, middle and the end of this book to write my book report." This became my go-to method of completing similar assignments.

Although these acquired skill sets, especially the negotiation skills, would prove useful later in life, they were a disadvantage while I was in college. I went into the environment with a preconceived notion of academia. Embedded within me was the young boy whose public-school experience would be the only reference for how to behave, causing me to take on college in an identical fashion. The only exception to this was that – so far – I was mature enough to exclude the bite that was so damaging. The temper.

This approach turned out to be not very smart, as it ended up producing the same behavioural response from my instructor that was so predictable from my grade-school teachers. My cutting corners and last-minute improvisation with presentations did not sit well with the instructor, a peace-loving, hippie-like lady who wore multi-coloured, maxi-length dresses, with accessories like beads and funky bracelets. In fact, she was so concerned about my juvenile approach that she decided to prevent me from going out to work on a practicum. Instead, she had me come to her class everyday while my classmates enjoyed a work experience that aligned with what they wanted to do for a living. She said, "John, I don't think you are ready to step out into the working world."

Instead, we worked on a business plan for a business I wanted to get going, a computer archival company. This "improvised practicum" was a sobering wake-up call for me. I realized I had some growing up to do. I recall being hard on myself, saying, "John, what are you doing? You are way more mature than this – it's time to man up!"

Academically, I did manage to do well despite my immature approach. But perhaps the greatest lesson for me was that there was no one to place the blame on. My mother's wise words helped me see that I and I alone must accept responsibility for my disasters, and purge my past, grow up and continue to think about my future." When you act like that, what kind of future can you expect?" she said to me many times during my first year at college.

Dominated by My Inner Child

The biggest thing I can take away from my first year in terms of personal growth? That the human services philosophy was that in order to look after others in the helping field, you must be mentally healthy yourself. There were a lot of assignments that compelled me to face my inner self and work towards personal improvement based on reflection.

Although it was a mentally exhausting venture, I learned more about myself in my first year than I have ever learned in my life up to that point. This growth was like a transformation, and by the time the year was done, I had learned just how much my inner child had dominated my adult life. The biggest revelation, however, was learning that this deep-seated angry child was key to surviving the world around me.

When I was young, I had no idea what was ravaging my happiness and as a result, my public-school days were spent just trying to make it day by day. And in doing that, I was reacting to my environment. The anger that originated from the deep-down and inexplicable hurt within, became the go-to emotion for defending myself against what I felt was unfair treatment by those responsible for my future. I didn't know how to communicate my defence so, like everything in life, I reacted in the only way I knew how – through screaming and yelling.

All this soul-searching in college had made me realize that I was still coping using the same old methods, trying to avoid, push down or otherwise run from the lonely and the sad. Or having the hurt inside manifest itself as anger. And me, not acting on it but being negative and otherwise hateful. True, I was happier at that time I was in college, but there was then, and always was, a dull sensation of sadness hiding just below the surface.

Once I learned that using ancient methods such as anger to avoid my inner pain was nothing more than a defense mechanism, I was then able to start growing. I was slowly letting go of that little fair-headed, blue-eyed boy and freeing myself, bit by bit, from those feelings of being small, weak and vulnerable.

Second Year: Addictions Counselling

In spite of some significant setbacks, such as missing out on my first-year practicum in college, I still had learned some valuable lessons. Mainly, I learned that it was time to put the little boy inside to bed and start to redefine myself as the adult I was growing into, whether I liked it or not. I wanted this, and wanted it badly, so it became a matter of "What do I have to do to get it?"

In an instant, all the "nagging" my mother did when I was a teen came flooding into my head. "You want to do well? Then open the damn book!"

Actually read? "Okay," I said. "I'll do that." Not only did I do just that, but I also budgeted time to study and completed the majority of my assignments. This new me is what I was determined to maintain in my second year where I was enrolled in addictions counselling.

But perhaps what helped me the most was falling in love with the course from the first day I landed in the classroom. I remember vividly telling myself "I love this, all of it, learning about addiction and psychology, crisis and best counselling practices – give me more." Learning how to actively listen, and the theory behind the variety of psychotherapies, was equally fascinating.

Finally, for the first time in my life, I felt like I was where I belonged. All the inner strife seemed squelched by this burst of passion for the field of counselling. I remember thinking to myself, "Okay, kid, man, this year is going to be the year I get to enjoy the comfort and stability this clarity of purpose has brought." Oh, my God, I remember thinking – so this is what it's like to feel calm, to have this feeling of calm wash over me, and all through the year.

What a bloody novelty! Where some of the students there might have revelled in parties, I revelled in the feeling I interpreted as "normal." It felt good, and the best way to describe it is a mild and consistent sense of euphoria.

This would be one of two moments in my life that I would experience such a feeling of inner peace. I did learn, that year, a lot about my own personal tolerances. If it weren't for standard social pressures, placed on young adults, I would have continued along this path of content.

With this newfound satisfaction came a new and powerful desire to learn. As a result, I soaked up every bit of what there was to take in. Learning the skills of the trade, those of how to conduct a counselling session through empathy, refection, and the power of silence, also fascinated me. It seemed that once I caught the learning bug, I would seek out all there was to learn about the human condition. I was reading study after study on what makes us tick, an obsession that still burns out of control to this very day. "My God," I said to myself, "I am in love. In love with the craft!" It was a tough course, designed to match the challenge level of university, and it not only fostered my love for knowledge, but was a final vindication, proof that I was not that learning-disabled young kid they thought I was.

Although I did well with the academic portion of the program, my head instructor had concerns about my learning style. I have never been able to learn by doing two things at once, so I chose to sit and focus on what was being taught, rather than to take notes. I could just imagine her saying, "This fella is not interested, and he's wasting my time." In reality, I had nothing on the desk because I knew how distracted I would be if I had a notebook open, trying to write things down. I always looked at it as an adaptation. I was always so full of anxiety that a singular focus, as I learned over time, was best for me. In this case, it came down to listening to what she had to say.

Perhaps her concerns were formulated on a traditional learning model that says learning occurs in all people the same way. Although I can't swear that this was her motivation, she was concerned enough to have me come to her office.

Appearing at her tiny office, I took a seat in a chair right at the side of her desk. With no idea why she had summoned me to see her, my anxiety was high. I had poured myself into catastrophizing the entire scenario well before my butt had landed in that chair.

My instructor, a shortish rosy-cheeked blonde woman, and who seemed to have an amiable wit about her, looked at me. But there was no smile. She began to talk to me and out of it all, I remember this: "It's my opinion, John, that the field of counselling probably isn't for you."

Remember the phrase, "You can't do that"? Well, as she spoke, the little boy in me reared its head from its hiding place and brought out all those feelings of uncertainty and lack of confidence.

She cited her reasons for believing what she had told me. As far as I could tell, her conclusions were based on the fact that I never opened a book and never took a note. It seemed like a leap to me, and my defense was: "I really do love the course, but I really struggled to take notes and hear what you have to say at the same time, and I missed too much." My words fell on deaf ears.

I ended up asking her in a defensive tone, "What are my marks like?" They were good, so I watched as – I'm sure – she tried to regroup and find another reason. I always felt this whole thing was more personal than professional. We often had discussions in class about domestic violence, a subject that piqued my interest. I noticed that the conversation was geared towards women only. I do recall asking her, "What about abuse towards men? I am wondering because I need to know how to best help this population." A perfectly legit question, so I thought. It got little response.

This year, I would go out on a practicum – that practical section of a course of study – but because she apparently was convinced I would be incompetent, she sent me out on a job placement that was not addictions-related at all. Upon learning of her plan for me, my claws came out and I went to see the department head, her boss. I told him what had taken place in her office and told him, "I don't understand why I can't go into the addictions practicums. My marks are good, and I've worked really hard."

Like the conversation I had with my instructor, my case to the department head fell on deaf ears. It felt as if he moved to side with my instructor. And my powerless attempts to change her mind landed me in an organization that helps people with learning and mental disabilities. This deflated me a bit, but I remained determined not to be taken down by their – as far as I was concerned – outlandish and unfounded approach. I was stronger because I finally knew my worth and what I was capable of. I just thought and said "I'll show them." However, I'd be lying if I said their decision didn't spin me out of control. Despite being determined not to have it cause a major psychological setback, I would find it ended up having an impact on my mental well-being, with some nasty consequences.

My initial reaction to my instructor's fateful decision? Devastation. I remember lying in bed, ruminating on the two meetings. "Why am I always getting the short end of the stick?" Yet, once again, I would get over that hurdle of anger and frustration (how many times can one hold it down?) and venture into the placement with an open mind. So, I had to do this – and as it happens, I quickly fell in love with helping this population to live their best lives. It turns out that I did show them, by picking myself up, dusting myself off and saying to myself, "Let's do this."

It was one of the most memorable experiences of my life. I would find myself living in a house with the people who lived in the home, and I would be there for six days a week, twenty-four hours a day. Tough, but I found I had a knack for caring for the sick and the vulnerable, and I developed a deep sense of compassion for those with mental and physical difficulties. That feeling was echoed by my superiors. Finally, I was being recognized, not for my challenges but for my authentic, caring and sensitive self. That was what I had been yearning for so strongly since I was a child.

I would stay on for a bit after I graduated from college, but the huge time commitment was too tough on both myself and my newly-formed relationship. We had decided that if we were going to start a life together, eventually, of course, this job would simply be too much for that, so I told her, "I will apply at the rehab Centre" – not ten minutes away from where we lived. This residential setting was home for those with cognitive delay, high-care needs, and behavioural challenges. I said to myself, "Working there would be perfect – an hourly wage job, I'm doing very similar work, and it has the potential of benefits and paid vacations."

Although I loved the work and it was difficult to walk away from, I had to do what was best for me. Working with all the wonderful people living there did help me with one thing: it opened one door when another was forced shut by yet another educator. With a newfound sense of purpose, I knew that I wanted to continue my career "helping those who have difficulties helping themselves," as I said it. I would devote nearly twenty years to helping this population with everything from their personal-care needs, to coming up with plans to minimize their problem behaviours.

And though it took a toll on me both mentally and physically, I feel very privileged to have had the opportunity to help try to improve their lives. On the days where the environment erupted into violence, which was often the case, it felt like you were moving backwards. But on the days where I helped talk someone down from a potential aggressive episode, I said to myself, "This is the most rewarding job. I love it here."

And initially, the rewards outweighed the stress. The relationship-building and personal care was a very cohesive experience for me. "If it weren't for us helping our folks with their daily lives, who would?" I often found myself saying.

CHAPTER SIX

The Real World

"The two things that made me grow into a man were college and of course, the fire service. I would later come to learn that I was ill prepared for either."

Passion! I took this new one – after successfully graduating from the Addictions Counselling program – and headed straight back to my workplace assignment, only this time as a casual employee. It provided me with a small income while I was looking for something that would allow me to kick-start the life we as humans often are primed to pursue.

How College Prepared Me for Real Life

What did college do for my mental health? I have thought long and hard over what were the things contributing to my newfound normalcy, and I have settled on a few potential answers. What likely helped provide the ultimate answers to this stability I had enjoyed during my college years were two things: finally having personal control over my own destiny, and the realization that I had a threshold of tolerance that is not quite as robust as others.

After years of having others take the wheel of my life's journey, I was thrust into adulthood and left to carve out a life for myself. Although I had entered the great unknown and I was fearful, I realized that I was free of the shackles that were slapped on my dreams growing up. Once I had established a sense of purpose in life and went to college, the great unknown was transformed into the beautiful land of opportunity.

As I completed each goal, my happiness and self-esteem were growing, really growing.

It wasn't until after college that I realized that my resilience and ability to take on real life were not up to the task that adult-ing is all about. When I was immersed in the structured world of higher learning, my expectations and daily routine were predictable. It even felt "cozy."

My second year was further away from the tiny town I grew up in, so I had little choice but to rent a room close by the college campus. Being a student living on a loan, I naturally looked for the cheapest place I could find to lay my head.

I found a boarding house for as cheap as I could get, and the living environment reflected the price. When I first stepped into the room I had been assigned, it was like I had entered a time machine and set the dial for the 1970s. It was the size of the standard bedroom, with pale green walls, a two-tone yellow-brown carpet, and a closet. The house had multiple rooms for rent, with a shared kitchen and bathroom.

Fortunately for me, there was only one other person living there, a skinny fellow with long brown hair, everything about his appearance also screamed "the '70s." This little rooming-house in the middle of the country provided me with a refuge. It had a simple environment and a beautiful silence that helped stave off my mental-health woes. It gave me a good balance to experience – between the stressful learning of the college and this stillness my living quarters blessed me with.

Then Real Life Happened

My successful departure from my college pursuits would come with its own set of valuable lessons. One of them was that I needed a reset and silence to maintain my positive and happy outlook. I first came to understand that this wasn't an optional thing for me. It was a necessity. This need for "down time" would continually prove to be true as my then-partner – who later became my wife – and I tried our best to make a go at life.

We followed the template that many people before us pursued: getting married, buying a home and having children. However, I soon found that this so-called "fairy-tale life" was just that, a tale. In reality, it was non-stop working, dealing with the challenges that come with being a parent and at the same time, trying to keep to a solid and loving relationship. The grand total of all this was hell on my mental health.

By the time my partner and I started our life together, I landed the job I was hoping for at the Rehab Centre. I was so happy to have been hired on here. It felt as if life was starting to come together. I recall saying to myself, "This could be my dream job." It was the ultimate opportunity to make a difference for people with high needs, and carve out the "dream" life I knew I had to live.

So, here I was, gone from a very hurt little boy with his own challenges and who never had any answers – to a sad reclusive teen riddled with anxieties – to a man who in spite of it all, had achieved the life many thought I was destined to fail at. Finally, I had beaten them all. The teachers, the doubting instructors, even the mental pain that plagued me all my life. And maybe most importantly, my acts of appropriate defiance showed me I could do it. I conquered my fears and in doing so, had let my authentic self out – unleashed and out the door. Well, to a certain degree, for someone who was inherently sensitive and a born helper through and through...someone whose passion, once cultivated, gave me the strength to say, "John! Be who you are!"

Can you believe I was incredibly happy about what I had overcome? Finally, the life I deserved was my reality. At the time I was convinced that this adult life I had earned was the driving force responsible for burying all the pieces of me that were the elements causing me so much distress and mental pain. That's what it felt like, being entombed.

It seems I was right to assume so. My ability to enjoy my younger adult years was extraordinarily strong. I played the role of husband, father, and full-time employee with enthusiasm and at a constant level of high energy. But like hailstones hitting pavement, the stressors of this life would start to crack the burial place I had built around my mental health. It would chip away at me until my "structure" would weaken and this pain inside force its way out of the cracks and once again, hold me hostage.

The Re-Emergence of Mental Illness

Surprise – the real world turned out to be nothing like the fairy-tale template I was led to believe it would be. Real life is nothing but running and working at everything. Your relationships, the constant upkeep that comes with home ownership, and of course the constant chasing of children. Because the nature of my work was caring for people with high needs, coming home to little ones – with their crying, constant noise and diaper changes – denied me of that all-important downtime I knew I needed.

Then there was the other stuff, the vehicle breakdowns and other things and events that needed immediate attention and money. To top it all off, I spent much of my time working seven days a week, a brutal schedule for working in a mental institution. Looking back, I see I worked so hard to pursue my dreams, passions and achievement of sustainable happiness.

The dream I had fought so hard for, this grownup "dream life," ended up as a nightmare for me, it was like trying to walk through a windy freezing rainstorm and getting pelted in the face by its tiny stinging frozen shards. After a while, you're literally sick of its sharp and unrelenting assault. You're finished.

Over time, I would feel the anxiety and sadness completely break through the walls of protection I had constructed, and it just started to consume me once more. As this grown-up reality stripped me of my sense of control, they came out again, like the awful imps they were – the mental illnesses.

More Than I Had Bargained For

Looks like life had turned out to be much more than I had bargained for. As a result, most of my young adult life was spent slowly becoming sicker and sicker. I was quick to become agitated and obsessed over getting things done, and was filled with more and more worry.

From what I thought was an overly dirty windshield to yelling at my wife because I was trying to fix one of the vehicles, it felt like a kind of simmering keg of dynamite. I was just so anxious and reactive in those days. But I still couldn't see the severity of what was brewing and igniting just below the surface. "Why can't I ever catch a break?" was a common thought back in those days.

The only good thing I had at the time was resigning from the fire department when my son was born. My decision to resign was like this relief valve that let out some of the internal pressure building at the time.

"I want to take the time for my son," is what I said then. Who wants to appear as broken or weak? However, I was also learning that I had become ill-equipped to deal with the darker side of helping others. I crumbled like the twin towers after the events of 9/11 when three hundred and forty-three of my fellow firefighters lost their lives. I was crumbling towards the ground and to certain devastation. I wish I would have known that at the time.

I see now, my decision to leave was more about saving myself. "How could I not have been aware of this?" It didn't occur to me at the time because the suffocating angst I was experiencing was not as familiar to me then as it is now. All I knew was that something had to give. "My son deserves a present dad," I often said to myself.

It was this moment in history that turned my "perfect life" to dust. Despite leaving the fire service, I already had a permanent injury. I wasn't aware of the extent of the damage then, but I can see it plainly now.

It would turn out that the fire department wasn't the only aspect of my life that was playing hell with my well-being. My dream job, working at this long-term care facility, ended up causing some major inner turmoil. The constant verbal and physical assaults – the unrelenting noise and running to help 26 individuals with their daily routines – was whittling down my positivity. Every physical assault and verbal altercation chipped away at my sense of safety. This is why my love for the job became an intermittent flicker until one day it went out forever.

"What's wrong with me? Why is it so hard to go to work now? It was so easy before." My constant heightened alertness replaced my love of helping the residents, with constantly fearing them.

I would learn that this dream job and my inner chaos were incompatible. Never knowing what I was getting into, I found that walking through the door was torture, and on more than one occasion I walked into my workplace and straight into a combative, screaming client in full-blown crisis. This was like a constant source of fuel that kept my anxiety alive and growing.

Looking back on it, I knew the path I had chosen in life had been both one of social expectation and suited to help fulfill my passion to help others. However, there was that self, the inner self, that was being robbed of a voice. I guess with each act of violence, my compassionate, highly-sensitive self felt like it needed to run and hide. All in an effort to save itself.

There's always a time to pay a price, it seemed, and within less than a decade, I would pay a huge one for ignoring both my own personal inner voice and the familiar, always-growing dread I had gotten to know during childhood. "What is happening to me?" While I knew the feeling well from the events as a child, I was unprepared for the adult version – stronger and more overpowering. I feel now that I just shut down mentally and was on autopilot.

It was a life that consisted of going to work, coming home – and catching up with the ever-longer to-do list. At this point, my first day back to work was daunting. I remember it well. The closer the hours got to my leaving for work, the heavier my entire body, inside and out, became.

CHAPTER SEVEN

Breaking Point

"Although deep down I knew I was suffering, the voice of society, ever-present, kept telling me to man up."

Mental illness is like carbon monoxide, that tasteless, odorless gas that slowly accumulates in the body causing health issues or death if left untreated. My anxiety disorder, although yet to officially be diagnosed, was slowly accumulating to the degree that I began to be symptomatic. Almost as if my angst started to radiate from the inside out, I began to feel it physically. Overtime my eyes began to twitch, and I began to feel sharp but short-lived pain shoot through my arms, legs and feet.

I had no way of knowing at the time that it was my mental health behind it, but I do recall saying "Something's wrong here. People don't go months and months with both eyes twitching." Once it became physical, I started to wonder if it was stress-related. Especially when the body pains became unbearable.

"Life has shackled me to a dream machine," I said to myself. "A machine producing the repetitive same old, same old." And just like with carbon monoxide, I failed to recognize how severe my illness was, leading to a decline. I felt myself poisoned to the degree of "do or die." I had reached my breaking point.

By the time my daughter was born on a beautiful warm day in June 2007, I had hit a critical point. Despite this, I felt it was "normal" to keep on keeping on: bed, sleep, work, eat and repeat. But I had detached myself from the rigours of life, ironically, so I could fool myself into thinking I was living it.

Stoking the Fires Within

While I was pretending to live the dream, I was unwittingly stoking the fires of mental illness. It would turn out that my insistence to live the modern concept of the dream life was a bit like setting up the damp conditions mould needs to grow and thrive until it makes a living environment untenable.

A few years later when my daughter was just a toddler and my son had started in big school, this constant repressive state numbed me from the inside out, like an emergency shutdown switch, its function to ensure my survival.

And it was at this critical junction, that I joined the fire department once again. This time, it was all a mistake and added no value to my life whatsoever. Whereas in the past, the fire department embedded some of the most important lessons of my life, this round was nothing short of catastrophic for me and would add layers of complication to my rapidly deteriorating mental health. Jumping back into firefighting was met with this mental-shutdown switch with every call.

One of my first calls back was a cardiac event which found me trying to perform CPR on an elderly man who didn't make it. The traumatic feelings that had shoved me out the door the first time round, reclaimed me with just as much ferocity as when I left. Only it didn't take years for me to feel its wrath. All it took was a beautiful warm spring evening and my first tragic call.

I should have known right then that I was only walking back into the same torture chamber I had freed myself from years earlier. Yet despite knowing I was in trouble this time around, I kept going. "John, you must be a sucker for punishment," was what I said under my breath many times.

Looking back at it, I say to myself, "Yeah – retrospect would have been a great tool to have at the moment I walked back through the doors of that fire station. If so, I could have seen what was the perfect storm that was coming for me." And I did sort of, I just felt that my five years of absence would have given me enough time away to somehow build a "stronger tolerance."

Here I was, working in this violent, loud and unrelenting environment, and barely in a marriage that was suffering as a result. Going back into the fire service could have only one of two possible outcomes: either I get off this train and allow my authentic self to take control and do what I must to survive – or I meet a premature fate that saw my life coming to an end.

I felt myself slowly being brought to my knees. I ended up being ill more often, calling in sick frequently. I was also starting to seek out isolation as a way to cope and escape the overwhelming world. "I can't do this." That phrase echoed in my head. I had grown up with a similar sentence, "You can't do that." Now, or so I believed, the "I can'ts" were beginning to become true.

"Maybe they were right after all. Maybe all those teachers and instructors knew that I was sick," my voice seemed to echo, and why not? It was going many years back.

My anguish would get to the point that I would go to work, to a multi-room living unit that consisted of a ten-to-twelve four-bed sleeping quarters. Each room ran down both sides of a long hallway, with every excuse to leave down the wide hallway and out the locked main door. At the end of this hallway were male and female bathrooms, a nursing station and a day-room.

After the clients went to work, to their respective day programs, I would hide out in the client's male washroom for at least an hour. It was the least likely place that I would be discovered. I was losing my ability to contain the mental-illness monster that was beating its way to the surface, and this cold porcelain glass-and-steel setting was becoming my refuge.

If it was a war here, I was losing it – this war with the self. And damn, I thought I had won it years before. This resurgence I was experiencing wasn't limited to this work environment. Instead, every aspect of my life was being weathered away.

Boiled to the Surface

Even though this war of the interior was initially a personal one and because I couldn't contain it forever, the casualties were inevitable. My family would be the first to experience the results of unchecked, untreated mental illness. As time went on, I became less able to tolerate the noise of my children, often overreacting to what was normal, age-appropriate behaviours. I often wonder "Why do all toys today make so much noise?" This constant barrage of singing, beeping and bopping, combined with what should have been innocent laughter, ignited the same mental-health fires that burned at work. Often becoming agitated by their play, I would yell, "Shut up – go do something else!"

The behaviors I was exposed to at work had a lot of similarities to those of my children, loud and constantly in need of something. I simply felt like I couldn't get away, And the engine that drove my mental intolerance never had a chance to cool.

I loved my job, and I loved my children but the scenario that was now mine denied me the opportunity to reset and recover. I needed quiet, I needed to retreat. Society contradicts this fact, and society didn't care if it was killing me. It just kept coming and coming. To get a bit fanciful here – it was almost as if it knew that I would succumb to its will if it just kept beating and pounding on my fragile disposition.

And so, just as my interior war had set me on permanent guard for whatever lay next, my partner had to brace for what was coming from me in real time. She was bearing the brunt of a fire I could not contain.

It wasn't uncommon for me to overreact to a simple request or the initiation of an innocent conversation. I was reactive, so was she. I was losing myself to the numbness and reactivity that I now know was trauma. This almost out-of-body experience came out of my life's choices and the constant death and destruction that came with those themes.

And it gave her a walking-on-eggshells kind of life. I had been consumed by this family dream world. But between constantly labouring to keep it all afloat and having a low tolerance from mental illness, it all somehow morphed together. And it tore up the pages of my fairy-tale life, leaving me no choice but to write a new life story. It would be one that would see me making a go of it on my own.

CHAPTER EIGHT

The Dawn of a New Beginning

"I knew that if I was going to get better, I had to double-down on my philosophical doctrine – do whatever it takes to get better."

It was something of a monster, this burden, and it was eating its way through me. I felt overtaken and consumed by my ills. And there I was stuck at that fork in the road. It felt a moment – maybe what they call a pinnacle? – where something just had to give. I needed peace from the war or would become a casualty from it.

I had been so consumed by my anxieties, so debilitated within my new reality, and I agonized over the decision I had to make, but found I had come to a moment of clarity. I could see the billboard-sized writing on the wall. "You're going to hurt yourself or worse if you keep going with a dream that's really not for you."

Fortunately, I understood I was facing life or death., My philosophical doctrine began to nag at me. "Do whatever it takes to get the job done," played continually in my head. And then "How are you going to survive?"

Once the tools that were so effective for me in the very beginning of my adult life were dusted off and reapplied, I was able to see the direction I must take. After all, I had two young and beautiful children to think about. I realized that I was quickly approaching a new dawn, a fact that came to me one night as I lay in bed so full of mental pain that I was bursting at the seams for some relief.

I can vividly recall getting up out of bed one sleepless night, entering the hallway, and collapsing into a sea of uncontrolled crying, and saying in between sobs, "I can't do this anymore."

As I lay there, stricken with pain so intense it poured out of my eyes and onto the floating floor beneath me in the form of tears, I understood why I had finally erupted like an inflamed spleen. I knew that I had come to the end of the road. In that moment, I knew I was in a full-blown mental-health emergency. What some call "hitting rock bottom." It would be almost a year before I would close the door on my world as I knew it. I needed a plan and time to execute it.

A Storm Before the Change

"That's it," I said. "The final piece holding my personal life together – now, finally disintegrated, leaving me trapped in its rubble." I had resigned myself to the fact that mental illness had successfully entrapped me. As a result, all I wanted to do was give up. And why not? Mental illness had not only trapped me but beaten me. Hadn't it?

Then I realized that I was not ready or willing to live by the conditions set out by sickness and social expectations. With it weighing on my mind constantly, I slowly began to see what I had to do to break free. As it happened, I had a plan thrust upon me by an incident one evening at work.

The night that changed my life forever by way of saving it, started with a very agitated resident and a well-meaning co-worker. In the months leading up to this fateful shift, I was barely able to walk through the doors at work. It was as though someone had constructed an invisible jelly-like substance just beyond the door, making my entry feel like I was walking through molasses. It's amazing how strong anxiety can be, making one feel so heavy that every step in life seems like an overwhelming task.

It so happened that on this shift, entering work was extra-tough. Evenings were always a challenging shift because all the residents were returning from their day programs. The noise and chaos always caused heightened agitation and behaviours for the folks who lived there. For a staff member, this was the time when you are most bombarded by a dozen requests. "It's my smoke time." "Can you open my locker?" "Can you play cards with me?" Many evenings there were three or four people requesting something all at once – hell, on an anxious mind.

These elements often caused tension and frustration for the clients because there were so many of them and so few of us. As a result, it wasn't uncommon to have a resident act out physically – and I found this especially for the ones who wanted their smoke. I always felt over-stimulation was a massive contributor to the evening shift. If we could feel it, the population that lived on this unit felt it ten-fold. They became "dysregulated," and their behaviours would easily escalate and explode as a result.

This evening, I too felt myself falling victim to the hustle and bustle taking place. As the ferocity of my anxiety grew, I often wondered how much longer I would survive in this environment. It was such a drain on me mentally that it was only a matter of time, I knew, before I had reached some tipping point. On this night, I could not handle the disarray that came from all sides.

Although I didn't know it at the beginning of the shift, I would find myself finally running out of track. The watershed moment that took me out like a sniper's bullet came when I was trying to provide intervention to a resident who was highly agitated and was known to be spontaneously aggressive. When I was in the midst of doing so, a colleague decided that it was appropriate to add what was essentially their own two cents worth. "No, John, you should be doing *this*." In doing so, they distracted me from my attempts at de-escalating the situation.

This was seen by the resident as an opportunity to strike me in the side of the head with his fist, ringing my bell and causing a white flash to dance before my eyes. My remaining composure snapped like a twig, causing my defenses against mental disorder to crack and crumble, releasing a barrage of hurt and anger, a warm feeling that hijacked nearly all my sense of control.

What I still find amazing to this day is that in that moment I had enough compunction to remain professional, long enough to escape the resident's bedroom. This well-meaning staff member was saying things like "Listen to John, he's only trying to help you." And "you need to calm down." I told her that it was okay and that I had it under control, but she persisted. "So are you going to listen to John?"

My level of anger was so high I couldn't speak till I emerged from the well-lit hallway and stormed my way into the four-by-eight nurses' station. The unit keys in my hand quickly met the desk with a clank, and in doing so caught the attention of my co-workers moving about the office. The only thing I remember saying was, "I'm out of here. I'm out of here." In a narrow-focused mindset, I charged like a bull, off the unit and to the supervisor's office where I yelled at her, "That's it, the end, I'm leaving. I don't care what the consequences are. Do what you will."

I remained there long enough to see the shock and surprise on her face and hear her say "Ooh-kay." Then I stormed out just as quickly and as angrily as I did when I busted through the heavy wooden fire door when I busted off the unit. I don't remember the drive home, nor do I remember explaining to my wife at the time why I was home early that night. I do recall her realizing just how serious I was about not returning there. Regardless of what she thought, as far as I was concerned the moment my keys hit that desk, I had given them my resignation.

The Call That Would Save My Life…Literally

When I rose the next morning, the fire in my belly re-ignited when about twenty seconds after my eyes opened, the fury came rushing back. The events that took place the evening before tumbled through my mind and before my eyes. My resolve to call it quits hadn't subsided. This came as a surprise to me. I traditionally have calmed down by the next day as logic and reason regain the wheel of my emotions and set me down that path to making amends. Those previous bouts of anger and conflict are something I usually deal with and feel sorry for.

But on this day, I felt this overwhelming sense of relief, so overwhelming that I felt good about my decision even though I considered I'd made it in a state of duress. It was a feeling of freedom, from the bulk of the weight I had been carrying for so long. "Gone," I said to myself. "Lifted, pulled off, dispersed. Gone." Days after the incident, I remained home whether I was scheduled to work or not, and while the anger subsided, the relief I was feeling from not being in that environment was like heaven on earth. I felt safe at home and that's where I wanted to stay.

On or about the third day, my phone rang. I answered to the voice of the Centre's director. I knew her as a tall fair-haired Registered Nurse who ran a tight ship but did so, I had found, with a boatload of compassion. Her voice was coolly professional, the conversation short. "Hello John. Come see me." This was followed by the familiar sound of an unbroken dial tone.

I was left with my mouth open. Being denied an opportunity to talk back, what else could I do? I said to myself, "Well, now I have to go see her." So, and begrudging it all the way, I made the trek to my workplace.

When I arrived, I was like a kid full of fear and uncertainty. Her phone call, abrupt as it was, had left my head swirling with all kinds of worst-case scenarios. Entering the lobby, I found a low-back chair and took a seat. My eyes wandered over to where she would emerge from her office, located just down the corridor, wide and well-lit.

Five minutes after my landing in the chair, my head was afire and I convinced myself that this meeting was going to be a sorry affair, met with disappointment on her side. A grown man was sitting in the chair, trying to play it cool, but inside, the ten-year-old me was bracing for a swift and severe punishment. Just as I was about to burst with overwhelming emotions, I heard "John, come on into my office."

The butterflies in my guts fluttered to the point of an awful kind of chorus. All I could muster at the time was a shaky "Hello."

Stepping in through the door of her narrow office, I was surprised to see a union-shop steward sitting there in a typical office chair parked directly in front of the director's dark brown desk. This representation from the union in the meeting made it feel like the purpose of the meeting was "disciplinary action." And despite having made up my mind that I had resigned, the emotions now churning through me felt like what I had always imagined being fired would feel like.

In a gentle voice, the director said, "Please take a seat – yes, in the chair next to her.".

I sat down and turned my attention to the industrial-grade, four-by-four-square floor tiles, focused on them. And all the time I was waiting to see my made-up, anxiety-driven fantasy of being let go come to fruition.

"All right, John," said the director. "I'd like you to tell me what happened on that last shift you were working."

I did my best. I really wanted to explain to her, rationally, what had taken place that evening. But that was battling with the conviction they were here to terminate me. I recall trampling over my words like a crowd fleeing a scene of chaos in desperation.

Once I had finally cleared the way for the story to roll off my tongue, I explained it all. Listening with great focus and attentiveness, she then said, "Why did you react that way?"

That simple question was like setting off dynamite on a dam. My whole adult life's mental struggles and personal pain all came flooding out and onto the airwaves around us. I still remember the look of compassion and empathy flooding her face and eyes. I knew right then and there that this was a meeting of support, and realizing this, I melted and cried with utter relief.

As she sat there silent and allowed me the opportunity to have the floor, I recall feeling the emotions rise to the surface, causing my voice to crack as my words fought and beat their way out. It was a rare moment for me. I allowed myself to be vulnerable and in doing so I laid it all on the line. There I sat, perched on that utilitarian chair, quivering with the relief of it, explaining that there was something deep inside that grew to dominate me at that time.

I felt as if my undiagnosed mental-health condition, the unrelenting stress that came with "living the dream" and the constant exposure to death and destruction, had been beaten around into one large vat of despair for most of my adult life. Like that of the atom bomb, the correct enrichment was all it took to ignite the doomsday device that ticked away in my head and in my heart for so many years.

The evening I made my escape from the centre was the ignition switch. From that moment on, I would be forced to renegotiate my relationship with a lifelong enemy. It was an enemy I would soon stand face to face with. "I know," I said to myself, "that whatever is wrong, needs to be fixed.,"

I felt as if she sensed that in this moment, she saw a man near the end of a life he wasn't designed for. I also felt as though she knew that my situation was so dire that something needed to be done. With tears in her eyes, she confirmed my conclusion, that this meeting wasn't a disciplinary one. Miraculously, the opposite happened: "John, you are a great employee, and this is not for you to quit, but rather you should take all the time you need, and your job will be waiting for you when you return." With her words, my high-alert, anxious state instantly surged down to be replaced with a sweep of reprieve and relief. Finally, here was someone saying or understanding what was really going on in my troubled and lonely head. It was like seeing the sunrise for the first time, a huge relief from the darkness I had become accustomed to.

Her approach and compassion literally saved my life because like a relief valve that allows gases to vent off in a safe manner, it provided me with a form of psychological release. Her reassurance that "you are not in front of me because you are being disciplined but rather, because of the events that took place that evening," showed compassion and support.

I am thankful she was able to recognize this fact. And it allowed my mental pain to safely blow off just enough inner anguish to keep me alive.

That day, I left my place of work mentally exhausted but with a sense of inner calm. I also walked to my car knowing I was in uncharted territory. The only thing that was certain, was that what lay before me was the opportunity I needed to get myself back on the road to mental wellness. I remember sitting in my car for what seemed like an eternity, saying to myself, "Now what?"

She was the first person in my life to offer me the help I always needed. I would make every attempt to go back to my place of work because of her genuine concern and kindness. It made me feel like I was part of something great, and so I wanted to remain a part of it. Because of this fateful meeting, she is the reason I am here today. And; for that, I will be forever in her debt.

CHAPTER NINE

What Exactly Went Wrong?

"The only way I thrive is through solitude."

So...the stressors of my profession were no longer taking up space in my mind, and the clouds that enclosed me had lifted just high enough for me to see this: that, although I had been gifted with the powers of relief, I was aware it was a temporary fix. To find a true solution, I was once again going to use the opportunity to "do what I have to do."

I often say decisions are easy; it's the actions that are hard. But I choose to do it every time, and this means action is required. So, I set about to end my marriage and embark on the sea of uncertainty.

It ended as I imagine many marriages end. First came the agonizing talk, a conversation that no one ever thinks they will have before or after they are married. After all, it's supposed to be happily ever after, right?

This honest heart-to-heart understandably had caused pain for her that could not be avoided, yet was something I tried my best to minimize. Being as sick as I was at that time, it is hard to recall the conversation verbatim, but what I do recall I was letting her know that because of my mental health, the family life was just too much. "I'm just exhausted and I can't do this any longer." "It's all about work, the kids, and less and less about you and I."

This period of my life is like a blur for me. I liken it to tiny soundbites of a life I once knew. However, in a lot of ways that no longer feels real to me. But I do recall us agreeing that the realities of life separated our love to such a degree where we felt like strangers living under the same roof. Even to this day, it comes up from time to time, and either one of us can be heard saying, "I don't remember much about our time together. We were both going through mental health problems and we just grew apart."

After wading through the chaos of this conversation I took up quarters on the leather couch downstairs, with its mix of half kid's-playroom and half living-room. Add "setting of heartbreak and uncertainty." As I lay there at night on our brown leather sofa, staring at the ceiling, I could barely stand the darkness of the night. It somehow made the pain so much worse. I felt as if I had failed.

Whenever my mind is left to its own devices, it will always magnify the worst of my feelings and make me question everything. The nights I spent in the basement were no exception. "Am I doing the right thing?" played over and over again as if my brain was put on shuffle. I do recall being run down with the realization that my home was no longer my home, that my family would never be the same – I cried at night and avoided the awkward days that preceded the breakup. Yet, despite its heart crushing-weight, I told myself "I still know this is for the best."

I would remain sleeping in the basement for about a month. This was as long as I could handle the near-constant tension before I would move into an extra bedroom Mom and Dad had at the back of their house.

This became my home, these walls painted pale-blue all the way around, this ceiling bone-white, this floor of grey vinyl. It was a small space, but with my parents' love and support, I felt like I had a little piece of the world I could call my own. It wasn't much to the eye compared to what I had had, but this simple room had an immeasurable significance. It became the cornerstone of my brand-new life and recovery.

A few weeks in my new space, I was reminded of my college days, and remembered that simplicity is bliss. I had realized that, for me, less really does equal more. Here, it helped free me from my social expectations that in reality, few people I know thrive on. My parents' generosity to me in my time of need will forever be forged in my head. If it wasn't for them, I would have had nowhere to go. "Thank you, Mom, and Dad," I must have said a hundred times. They refused any money from me despite my best efforts. So, we came to a compromise: I did a lot of the housework and I made most of the supper meals.

The advantage or disadvantage of living in a quiet little room in the back of my parents' home for what was the best part of a year and a half, is that it created a form where my mind could be let off its leash and run wild. But unlike a dog running around, my brain seemed never to tire.

One of the central topics that dominated my neurological processes, as a therapist might say, was: just exactly what was my part in the demise of the life that I had worked so hard to create?

One of the recurring themes that surfaced was the notion that I might have PTSD. A thought so terrifying to me that I did what the fire service conditioned me to do, instantly push it deep down inside and deny it as a possibility. So, like a person trying to close a closet door filled with stuff, I held the thoughts of PTSD at bay and quickly slammed the door on there being any truth to it. "Nah," I would say to myself. "I'm not that guy."

But just because I couldn't see what was beyond this metaphorical closet door, didn't change the fact that there was still a disaster lying just beyond the other side. Sooner or later, I would have to face this mess that, as I know now, was post-traumatic stress disorder. My deep denial simply gave it full command over my anxiety, misleading me for what would be the best part of eighteen years. My refusal to acknowledge it only cultivated its power, like seeds deep down in loamy earth.

Near the tail end of this near 20-year denial, around or about two years before I went off work in 2019, I began to "feel" it. With my most recent encounters with death and its destruction, trauma's effect started to slowly boil to the surface like lava through a fissure in the earth. I went from, "Nah, I'm not that guy" to "Okay, you're barely keeping it together, there's definitely more going on here than a plain old anxiety disorder." Around a year and a half into that two-year stint, I was convinced that I had PTSD. "Man," I addressed myself, "After reading so much on PTSD, I can see it, I am pretty much the walking definition of someone with post-traumatic stress disorder."

When it came to the point where I was terrified and too mentally weak to show up to, well, to anything, I knew that I was heading into a type of chaos that would be across roads that felt familiar. My choice to give up family to save my life, and this newly emerging terror, felt similar. My previous life-saving experience served as the warning siren. Without it, I would surely have written my final chapter. Yet, despite my very strong suspicion and familiar feeling deep in my guts, I still refused to deal with it. After all, I didn't have time for such things because I had kids to raise.

The anxiety...now, that was something I was willing to concede to. Back then, I could easily entertain it as the major culprit for not only the disintegration of my most recent life, but also the producer of the hurricane that ripped through my childhood, too. Somehow that felt safer than the prospect of having PTSD and was something I felt I could work with. So, it must be the anxiety angle that was at the epi-centre of all my life's difficulties. To quote that composite therapist again: "The fundamental flaw with this assessment is that anxiety can manifest itself as its own condition or be a side effect of another mental health disorder."

Perfect! Because if it were true, then I could throw dirt on any other possibility and bury it so deep that I didn't have to deal with anything else. Whatever was doing the damage, was "whatever" – in the sense that I had to make a commitment to myself and therefore find a cure for my ailment. Or maybe it was ailments? Even though I had my suspicions, I wasn't sure. However, even though I didn't want to believe it, that I was suffering from more than one mental-health condition, it was something that came into my mind as a possibility. And not a welcome one. I felt I just couldn't take on any more hardship at the time. Either way, I knew I was going to have to eventually go to war with myself and bring forth those powerful and all-consuming burdens that lurked and smouldered in the darkest corners of my mind for too long.

Part of my commitment to getting better and back to work was therapy. My employer had an employee-assistance program, a program set up so you could access a counsellor at no charge. I first pushed that aside and stuck to my "philosophical doctrine" to do whatever I had to do to get better. In this case, despite how I felt, I had to push aside any fears and make the call for help.

A Barrier To Mental Care? Don't Care!

The prospect of asking for help was a terrifying one, and why that was, I can only speculate. I do know that I had gone through my entire life up to that point being told that men don't talk about how they feel, ever.

The closest I ever came in terms of sympathy from another man was, "Man, you'll be alright." Or "That's nothing dude, it will pass." These notions never made any sense to me. Even now, I can vividly recall saying to myself things like "But I need to talk, I need help!" Having always been trapped in my own isolation, this unwillingness to talk about men's mental pain somehow made this isolation seem even more lonely.

All this had ever done was create a chronic sense of awkwardness and internal conflict. Thus, for my entire life, with the exception of therapy when I was a kid, I remained silent while it grew and festered. So, as you might imagine, seeking counselling was huge, overwhelming, and irrationally very scary. Having spent a decade in the fire service by this point only added to the terror. Real men, real responders, aren't supposed to be this scared. "Man, I wonder how much longer I can keep doing this, keep lying to my colleagues, to myself?" I would mutter.

And as if all that fear weren't enough, being an overly-sensitive person didn't help. Highly-sensitive people tend to feel more intensely, and my own fine-tuned emotional interior had primed me to have a stronger desire to communicate my inner turmoil. Society's tendency to condition people like me to silence the pain, coupled with this sensitive disposition, made the suppression feel really bad...excruciating. I needed to talk. I needed release. But like that of a bird caught in a cage, forever being denied the opportunity to fly, I felt trapped. So much so, that I'm certain my troubles grew enormously, leading to this little bedroom in a quiet part of my parents' house.

Mostly though, I felt that somehow banishing the PTSD angle to the outer regions of my mind would somehow make me more of a man and therefore, any admission in my view was a sign of weakness. For years, I struggled with the definition of what it is to be a man. For instance, I once had one of my Fire Captains proclaim, "The fire service is where a boy grows into a man." I understood what he was trying to say, however deep inside I was still struggling with low self-esteem, so his statement sounded to me like I would never achieve this great status of manhood.

For nearly all my life, I have felt inadequate and small from statements like, "Oh boy, don't be so foolish!" "Suck it up and be a man!" So, I've resigned myself to the fact that I would always have to be silent. Being silenced in one form or another is all I've ever known. "I give up! I'll just keep quiet."

Despite being mentally just like me by all the social conventions of how a man should behave, I managed to get around this form of conditioning about my gender role and overcome any fear of saving myself. How? By acknowledging, saying hello, and laying a claim to my persistent and debilitating fear. That was all there was to it. So to quell the fires that were raging in my mind, booking my appointments regardless of how I was feeling, was a great example. When I think back on it now, I quickly learned that with every push back against this demon, I was one foot further down the path to wellness. This railing against what was really myself, opened my mind up to even more potential solutions. And even though the low tone of every man's voice I knew growing up still messed with my head, I was determined to push back against the negative narrative they had left behind, often saying, "I need to do the opposite of what they have said or didn't say."

With the cogs of my solution machine going full tilt, I started to draw up a wellness plan. It was a plan that would be multi-faceted and holistic in its approach, the only approach I felt would work. Fortunately for me, I am a research geek. If I am to tackle a problem, I figure out what techniques give me the best chances of success. My behaviours in those days had shown to me that I likely had a diagnosable mental illness. If this was true, what was it and how would I find out? In my endeavours to seek out the best approach, I found that combining the counselling with psychiatry increased the odds of getting better, more likely to heal with the correct diagnoses.

It seemed to me that the first step was to talk to my family doctor. After receiving the blessings of my director to take all the time I needed to get better, I made an appointment with the doc straight away. This short dark-haired woman with a brisk, even hurried disposition about her, was well aware of my history and potential psychiatric challenges. So, revisiting my mental health would be short and to the point.

I went in with the express purpose of asking for a referral to a psychiatrist. I was thankful that she said, "I really support the idea, John, and will send one off immediately." Although I felt my general practitioner was a great place to start, I knew it was best to see a mental-health professional whose specialty was diagnosing mental health conditions. If I was indeed sick, it made more sense to me to have them confirm it – and help me work towards a solution.

No Easy Feat

When you are staring down the barrel of a potential mental illness with a label attached, let me tell ya, it's very difficult to make that initial appointment. I failed to recognize how strong my own denial was around having a name to go with these out-of-the-norm behaviours. Not only in my young adult life, but very likely as a contributor to my woes ever since I was a child. It was a downright scary prospect. After all, "I am a man, a firefighter and therefore gifted with the ability to be immune to a psychiatric disorder. Right?" Wrong! This notion made up of half mythology and half ignorance of how humans actually tick almost cost me my life.

Along with my sense that there was something wrong, I also had a persistent feeling that the way we handle matters of the mind wasn't an effective strategy. It nagged at me, even after being shut down by the men in my life, and even today, I often find myself saying "This isn't right." For all the talk of the new man and sensitivity training, the behaviour and stereotypes continue.

Realizing that these inaccurate concepts designed to save us some sort of awkward interaction with someone of the same sex were so damaging, I knew this: that if I were to get to the bottom of what was plaguing me, I had to cast aside my "manly" disposition and call my local mental-health clinic. Done.

Once my appointments with a psychiatrist were finally made, I felt I should go one step further and seek the help of a counsellor. It took some time, but I actually called my EAP (employee assistance program) and cemented the deal. Securing the date and time on paper made it feel I had no choice. I was committed. "The first step in my plan, complete," I said to myself. That cemented it too.

After braving the phone calls and having the appointments set, I felt liberated in a sense, free from these traditional taglines and the cultural expectations that went with them. Perhaps the most surprising thing to me was how I felt after making my initial phone call. "My God," I said to the air. "I not only feel free – I feel empowered."

On my life's journey, it has become very important to me to embrace every moment of personal control I get – especially as I had so little growing up. Mostly, I have found that being able to choose my own fate is like a booster shot against, not only my childhood circumstances, but my lifelong struggle of not being in charge of my own destiny.

For me, being psychologically oppressed, not believed, and silenced since being a boy had real, long-lasting consequences. How well I remember the lines like *"Stop your bawling," "Suck it up!" and "Just keep yourself busy."* While the voices responsible for the pain these statements caused are a bit murky today, "stop your bawling" was a common one expressed by a variety of family members.

Hammered into my head for years, they became the gold standards in dealing. Now at the age of thirty-two, I understood that the inaccuracies of these standards had at least two very good outcomes. While it had backed me into a corner for years, it also compelled me to seek answers for my mental derailment as an adult.

With constantly being silenced and therefore oppressed in a sense, the second great thing that I've learned from my own journey is to stand up in defence of the weak and oppressed. "I can't stand seeing people suffer." I've said to many as I voiced my concerns of social injustices and wrongdoings by anyone from corporations ripping off their customers to governments making cuts to essential public services.

I had come to realize that the way men handle any wound psychologically was nothing more than a form of a home remedy for all of the mental discomfort that invades our souls. I consider myself fortunate to learn that not dealing accumulates more and more damage. As far as I'm concerned, "manning up" is nothing more than a scientifically unproven method of "dealing." Now though, I look at it as a sort of mental equivalent of snake oil, once used to "cure" physical ailments. Nonsense. Finally, I felt I was well on my way on my healing journey.

Reflection

As I suppose many people do, I often reflect on my life's journey and like a puzzle, I try to work out what bits got me to any given point. What was this picture I was constructing as I wandered through my life? At this juncture, I feel like when my head first hit the pillow on that homemade bed, built out of rough pine, at my mom and dad's house, that this puzzle had lost many pieces. Some had been forced into place by the brutality of my life experiences. If you don't talk about the death and destruction you have endured for years, then you have little choice but to construct a narrative you can live with. And that is whether this narrative is true or immersed in a sea of denial.

For a long time, I chose to deny. However, my survival was so crucial that engaging my authentic self in order to live to fight another day was what eventually took priority. Even now, I rarely cry, despite that I have grown to be okay with it. In fact, I often tell myself when I'm sad, "It's okay to cry."

I am not what you would call manly, at least not in the traditional sense – I simply pretended, like a character on TV. I simply can't deal with the horrors I have seen, nor do I have it in me to "get over" my lifelong battle with mental illness. Not now and as I come to realize, not then, either. I will always be grateful that I "manned" up. A real man or anyone really, quickly can learn what they are made of when they go head-to-head with their ill mind – and seek out the help they need to be reborn and to actually live, not merely stroll on through in survival mode. "Isn't overcoming one's inner demons the true measure of one's strength?" Or in more traditional terms, "manning up?" It's a statement I still replay in my mind, even to this very day.

Putting in the work has taught me so much, mainly how strong I truly am. I was wrong to believe that my woes would somehow be absorbed somewhere in some unmarked place within me if I just pushed it all down. "Man, I've come a long way, but I sometimes wonder if I will ever completely rid myself of this outdated concept of what defines a man." I remember making this statement to a male trauma counsellor years back.

His response? "It's what you do in the present that matters. Just keep working on you, and work within your own values."

Because of this tough-guy narrative, my courage to book these appointments and see them through did not come easily. I hated and feared the heaviness in my chest, the brain fog that obstructed my cognition and the fear that has so frequently accompanied me when I took on the unknown and left myself open and raw. But despite being uncomfortable, with these dreadful feelings, I learned to overcome them. Basically, I would "throw myself to the wolves," so to speak. For example, I'd make a note to call and commit myself to a date and time. I knew that once I did this, the chances of me wimping out were very slim. And when said date and time would come, I'd say with a deep breath, "John, you can do this. You have to do this!"

Once I started adding tasks like this to my calendar, it began to feel like, "It has to be done." Once this feeling started to lower the power of my anxiety, I would say, "Oh, it's Tuesday. I have to call to make an appointment to see my psychologist."

But when first embarking on the "doing whatever I had to" philosophy, I recognized that how anxious I was, was irrelevant. What mattered was getting better. While the feelings of dread tried to overtake me, I still mustered up the strength to make my phone calls and go to my appointments. When I needed an extra push because of the inevitable worse days than others, I would physically make a list of why I was committing myself to getting better. Chief among them was to be the best damn dad I could be.

Perhaps because my fate was so often in the hands of others, I eventually came to understand that "oftentimes, the world doesn't care about how you feel. Therefore, you must force your way through what makes you uncomfortable." After having this revelation, it became about moving forward for me and with that, I was able to make the calls. By coming up with a plan, I stopped being a victim and became my own mental-health warrior.

CHAPTER TEN

Conquering the Mountain

"At the base of this monster of a mountain was the very tough act of overcoming my strong father's instinct not to see my children in pain."

From the moment I finished booking my appointments with the mental health professionals, the waiting produced a whole new fantasy of worry. It was like I had these sickening caverns in my head, and yet another wave of anxiety rising from them. Therapeutically speaking you could call it another and another "negative script" to deal with.

Hitting the end button on my Blackberry, I felt filled up, like a big bucket, with so many mixed emotions. On one hand, I felt a sense of relief, as though I had finally found civilization after a lifetime of wandering through the desert. On the other, a fear washed over me, the feeling you get when you're really anxious about something but regardless, you know you have to face it. It's a bit like standing on stage-left moments before you must go on to perform. It's this brand of fear that, in everyday life, can make people sick to the belly. Yet many of us can push through it.

The difference between this brand of anxiety versus an anxiety disorder is that stage fright, for example, is a temporary and natural form of anxiety, whereas somebody with an anxiety disorder has continuous bouts of stage fright, often several times a day. This is often the go-to example I use to try to help people without anxiety understand it.

Now that my appointments were committed to paper, I saw them as that point in time where I was just about to hit the stage. "There's no backing out now," I would say aloud.

"And now let's lay out this sort of verbal contract with myself." I called it the "do whatever you have to do" contract.

There was no question that this was going to be a huge mountain to climb, but when there's no going back, and when you're fighting for your life, what other choices do you have? Living with my parents, everything was a hurdle. Seeing the kids was difficult because there was no place for them to stay, so my contact with them was sparse. I could practically chew and taste the disappointment. My daughter, a fearless and adventurous kid, was too young for school, so she spent every day with me and went home at night with her mother. Nearly every day she would look at me with those big blue eyes and say, "Daddy! Can we please watch *Caillou*?"

I felt sad most of the time because it seemed I was reduced from being her daddy to being more like her babysitter.

My son, a fair-haired boy with a love for cars and everything to do with them, was going to school at the time. He would go for drives with me and we would do what I called "Dad and the lad time" together, one-on-one time that I think gave us both something to remember. At the time – like the laughing so hard it hurts – it gave us just a good physical feeling – and for me, the heart is part of that. Going on adventures became our thing. As he jumped into the truck and buckled himself in, he would always say, "Dad, can we go to find more dead ends?"

"Sure, son, let's do this."

The Most Heartbreaking of Things

At the base of this monster of a mountain was the very tough act of overcoming my strong father's instinct not to see my children in pain. However difficult, I knew that I had to put them through some tough times. I also knew that no matter how badly it stung, it was best for everyone. Cruel to be kind.

My mental capacity at the time felt fragile as a spider web, and I knew it gave me a low threshold for stress and tolerance. In the case of my children, I wouldn't have been able to deal with the false hope that comes with blurring the lines of

Daddy's home and Mommy's place. The pain that it would have caused them on an ongoing basis, would have been so mentally taxing, I would have been so distracted by the pain. I would have failed them as a dad.

At the time, I felt like I was wearing a pair of custom-made cement shoes, that weighed me down with a feeling of dread as much as concrete. I did know that I needed to help my kids understand that Daddy wasn't coming back home. If I was going to minimize the impact on my children, I needed to make some personal sacrifices, decisions that gut me to this day. My goal was clear, to ensure they knew two things. One: it was not them I was leaving and two: that the breakup between their mother and me was not their fault.

Once again, I was faced with the old adage, "What do I need to do to solve this?" With my kids, I knew that if they were to have any chance at getting through this without blaming themselves for the rest of their lives, I had to do "whatever it takes" to ensure that they grew up healthy, well-adjusted adults. My desire to make sure that they at least had the resiliency skills to get through that confusing and emotionally trying time, had to trump any desire to contact them when they were with their mother. I also had to resist the overwhelming urge, almost a feeling of pain, to go and tuck them in at night. I remember lying there, in the stillness of night thinking "Have I made the right decision?" Every time my head hit the pillow, my heartache would make me question what I, deep down, knew was the right thing.

It was the hardest thing I have ever had to go through, countless nights missing out on bedtime stories and goodnight hugs and kisses, laughter that was never meant to be, and all because of decisions that I knew, in my own heart, I had to make. Although I knew those decisions were absolutely the right thing for my children, I will still never forgive myself for missing out on all those beautiful little-kid moments. Those moments that for a split second erase all the pain and stress of life and fill you to the brim with nothing but love and innocent joy, like it's just been pumped inside you or has exploded from within. I often wonder how the human body can hold it.

Those fateful decisions, the ones they had no say in, had saved my life and because of that, they have always had the father I wanted them to have and the dad they really needed me to be. Perhaps most importantly, we all learned that life doesn't care about how we feel sometimes and doing the right thing, no matter how heart-wrenching it can be, is almost always better in the long run.

Now that they are teenagers, I can see that the sacrifices I had made, the boundaries I had set, have done what I hoped it would do. I recall several times, my son would say "Dad, can you come home?"

A heartbreaking statement from my five-year-old, yet, with all my strength, I knew I had to say, "I'm sorry, son, but your mommy and I went from loving each other to being friends, friends who don't live together." When these sorts of questions came up, I would always end them with, "Even though Mommy and Daddy don't love each other anymore, my love is like that of a superhero. Indestructible."

They didn't end up hating me like I feared, and most importantly, it didn't cause any sort of irreversible damage to them. In fact, my young fella will, even to this day, tell me, "Dad, you have made me into the person I am today, respectful and caring. I really appreciate that."

My daughter and I spend a lot of time laughing and bonding over stupid humour. Wedged within this silly stuff are some pretty heavy conversations on social issues. "Dad, why is the world the way it is?" she often asks. "Dad," she says to me, "You're weird, but I love your dad jokes."

I built our family around a "we-are-all-in-this-together" type of approach. But in order for this to work, I had to do my part as a member of "team Arenburg." If either of them asked, "Dad, can you help me with cleaning my room?" I would say, "Sure, you helped me out the other day with the dishes, so let's work on this together too."

As I have watched them grow, I have seen that they are generally positive people. The proof is in the way I see how they conduct themselves. I have always told them to "Stand up for yourselves, and just as important, stand up for others who need help."

My boy, an empathic fellow who loves playing guitar and is always ready to lend a hand, is so respectful that he calls me out when I am rude, saying things like, "Dad, you raised me to respect everyone. I feel a bit disappointed when you are disrespectful to others."

My daughter, or "kid," as I often refer to her, now a 5'4" athletically-built young lady, is my little social activist and stands up for others and what she believes in. Both her mother and I have raised her to be strong and use her voice. Although she can be a little more inward than her brother, she will ask me things like "Why are people so mean? You have raised me to be good to others, so, I don't understand why people are racists or sexist." Her deep sense of justice has come to her naturally and she has used it to defend herself. I remember the time when the music teacher shoved her, she came to me and said, "Dad, what she did wasn't right, and I feel like I need to do something about it."

I responded with "What does 'do something about it' look like for you?"

She thought for a moment and said, "I could write a letter to the principal?"

"That's a wonderful place to start," I said. After showing her how to write a letter to the principal, she took it from there. I remember saying to myself, "Most of the adults I know don't have the courage to take on things like that." To watch her defend herself was amazing, especially so because at the time she was only 11.

One of the big lessons I have learned in my life is that of positive outcomes that rise out of painful sacrifice. "Life is hard, yet I have reason to get better," is one of my sayings.

Clearly, I had done what was best. It would seem that no matter how uncomfortable my "do whatever it takes" doctrine was, it paid dividends in the long run. As I worked on myself, I felt the fog lift little by little. I recall feeling more and more happy and less imprisoned by my illness. "I am so lucky to have this chance to turn my life around," I'd say to myself. Even as I write this, my thoughts turn to my former director, who told me on many occasions to "Take all the time you need."

My First Therapy Session

When the day came for my first session with the therapist, my anxiety was running high. My mind raced with endless possibilities as to how it would all play out. Oddly, I felt as if she was going to discover that I was somehow making it all up. After all, I had rarely been believed or taken seriously my entire life. The whole way there, I would just say to myself, "She's not going to believe me." She's going to think I'm faking it."

My anxious self took me back on a trip through time to the days when my so-called problem-child complex still dominated my character. The child in me, still thriving deep within, sees everyone in a position of power as someone who will punish rather than help. "I feel like a kid getting in shit for being ill, like always," I felt. Psychologists were no exception. In such scenarios, this inner voice was the dominant voice, seizing control of the day. This initial session set my anxiety on fire and as a result, my inner child was scared to death.

Sure enough, as I arose the morning of the appointment, the anxiety began to rise, and the dread became heavier. I remember crawling into my old clunky pickup, taking a deep breath and thinking about running back to bed. And then I thought to myself, "No! That's just the anxiety talking." I gritted my teeth, started the engine and made my way to my psychologist's appointment. This moment was significant because it was the first time I had pulled together the strength to brush my anxiety aside and do what I knew was best for me. I came to say to myself. "You have to do it. Who else will do it for you if you don't?" And "Remember John, this is do or die."

Once I located the office, I parked my old beater Chevy S-10 pickup in the parking lot and made my way to the entrance. With my anxiety topping out at a solid 8 out of 10, I had to push myself to enter the building and into the realm of the unknown. "First time since you were a kid," I said to myself, grinding my teeth. "First time you've been to therapy since you learned to spell." I saw words flash in front of my eyes, all the things I'd been told about who I was.

Yes, I was frightened at the prospect of confronting my inner turmoil as a grown man. I had to thank my experience with my first therapist for giving me the strength to at least try the session. This man, my first therapist, with his soft voice and middle-east inflections had, in some indirect way, continued to save me with his everlasting impact. He had helped make it easier for me to tolerate the anxious waits in the waiting room. It was as if he had pulled away some of my fears of what I was to expect from therapy.

Time has a way of causing memories to fade to black, making recall spotty at best. Because I was only a kid back then, my time with this talented social worker had become murky for me. So much so, that my memories were mostly missing of what took place, like a spliced-out piece of film whose content has become insignificant over the passage of time.

Finally, the moment of my truth would be revealed now to this woman when she called me into her office. Though I didn't know it then, it was the beginning of seeing one of the best psychologists I've had to date.

What little I can recall is that of a soft-voiced woman with wavy dark hair, her office busy with odds and ends, and with a cozy feel. The lighting set to a mild glow was very comfortable and made me feel at ease.

That day I first landed in her office – the most therapeutic setting I have been in to date – I was so heavy with despair that all I wanted was for it to end. As I have felt before, the options for lessening or ending this pain seemed to be so few that it was making more and more sense to me to put myself to rest, permanently.

Although my mind as I once knew it now seemed a stranger to me, I do remember feeling – by the time the therapist and I parted – that I had a new perspective on my life and its direction. Cognitive behaviour therapy, the model my psychologist used, has helped me to see the irrational speech that comes with anxious thought processes and negative self-speak. I know now that I have certain-one liners that can tell me if I am getting anxious. One of the more common ones is "No one likes me."

By challenging myself with a rational approach, I can ask myself questions that, over time, help me ease my anxious mind. The right questions are essential here. "So, is it possible that no one in the world likes me? Of course not." "Did I really do anything that made every person I know dislike me? This is likely not the case either." "I need to use such cues as a way of telling me who's in the driver's seat. My authentic self, or the monster I have gotten to know as anxiety." So, over my many sessions I learned to identify the feelings produced by this mental illness and stop it from dominating my mind.

I still think that the brain is an amazing organ. I often think about what I had learned in therapy, thinking, "Man, I'm glad I have this skill now, especially now that I have post-traumatic stress disorder."

My Psychiatrist
The Other Piece of the Wellness Puzzle and a Diagnosis Too

My psychologist wasn't the only miracle worker in my case. My psychiatrist, a ready-to-retire man of Egyptian heritage with a thick accent and thinning jet-black hair, was a lifesaver for me.

When I first sat down in front of him, I noticed how unremarkable his office was: a small, almost perfect square, made of cinder block all the way around. It sticks out to me because the place and its furniture reminded me of the 1980s.

Because there was little to no therapeutic intervention taking place, because his job was to figure out the right kind of medication for me, our interaction was pretty well the same.

So much so, it felt more as if we were getting together and rehearsing lines for a TV show. "How do you feel? Are you feeling better with the medication?" were commonly-repeated questions.

The only differences in the script came with the medication he prescribed and of course, the diagnosis he gave me. "You have a mild impulsivity issue, not diagnosable as ADHD but a mental disorder of the anxious variety, *generalized anxiety disorder*." I had limited knowledge as to what that was, but I was not surprised. After decades of struggle, this was more of a confirmation than something from the air.

When those words flowed from his lips and into my ears, my first reaction in my head was: "What exactly is generalized anxiety disorder?" So, in a rush, I asked him.

"John, it's when a person has an excessive feeling of near-constant worry about everything," he said. "The source of the anxiety is often unknown. Evidently GAD, as it is commonly referred to, can cause physical symptoms too, symptoms like shortness of breath, heart palpitations and more."

In an instant, I had a light-bulb moment. This was everything that was happening to me, especially at work. I literally thought I was dying when I was dominated by these symptoms, and that's something I've since read about, experienced by many, many people with anxiety, panic attacks, etc. I even had a name for this sense of worry – I had always referred to it as just me being a worst-case-scenario thinker. It was so much a part of me for so long, I thought it was a skill-set, not a mental illness. I had always believed that this "skill" was what made me a better firefighter. I could see how to minimize situations that were not safe, dangers that it seemed no one else could see. "Yes – I did become a master of something," I'd sometimes say to myself. "A master at predicting the potential outcome of dangers down the road if certain precautions weren't put in place to help reduce impact."

Now armed with a diagnosis, I had a clear sense of direction, a jump-off point from which I could really pave my way to wellness. I don't recall having any conflicting feelings. I just remember a sense of relief wash over me. "Finally, finally, it all made sense. I, John Arenburg, have not been just some over-reacting, hard-to-deal with fella, but rather, my insistent worry or GAD has been such a dominating force." Furthermore, I was so overwhelmed with it, that I really did need the time to reorganize my world into something that didn't exceed my tolerance. Or at least until I was better. "So, this is why I can't take on things like I used to," I said to myself.

From the day I got my diagnosis, my venture up this necessary mountain became so much easier. It was like the journey went from needing ropes and steel-and-aluminum carabiners with spiked shoes – to a well-groomed path that required only a good set of sneakers, and enough strength and stamina to navigate around or over some obstacles that lie over the trail.

CHAPTER ELEVEN

The Buck Doesn't Stop There

***"The greatest lesson I have learned from all this?
Action is required if one wants to get better."***

With a diagnosis on paper, a prescription in hand and some new tools to try to blast the negative self-speak that had been such a dominating force for so long, I recall saying, "Now, this is what hope feels like." Yes, some actual potential of finding freedom, my newfound freedom. Finally, it felt as though I had got this train wreck of a life and human back on track and could now start to boldly move forward. Coal in the engine, a hand on the controls...and time to roll.

While I had righted the ship with all the traditional treatment approaches, I knew that the medication element was something I didn't want to dominate my life. So, what did I have to do to ensure I could live my life without the need for pharmaceuticals? In the fire service, we are conditioned to be problem-solvers. So, telling myself, "there has to be a better way" came naturally to me.

Feeling like my thirty-something self had only half the solutions, I gave more thought to what my holistic plan would look like, a plan that would see me gain and sustain an overall sense of wellness without pills. That was the goal.

This is where my love for learning came in handy. Although being off work and having less contact with my children hurt, in an excruciating way, it did give me a lot of time to satisfy my love for learning and find the answers I was seeking.

Running: Mother Nature's Medication

This disposition towards learning would pay off, as I obsessively sought out all the links between better mental health and exercise on my tiny, mid-2000 BlackBerry screen. I was amazed to discover that there was a treasure trove of recurring themes within the bodies of literature I was squinting to read in this dimly-lit bedroom at my parents.'

Crammed within the not-so-credible pages of the internet, lay scientifically-valid health research. Contained within the black fonts and white backgrounds of these online science journals, I began to see commonalities among the different bodies of papers. While the focus of these research papers may have differed in the subject of study within the realm of mental health, their findings were coming to similar conclusions. For example, when I searched for *exercise and anxiety* and clicked on the results, somewhere within the body of work would be the benefits of running, I saw this when I researched overall mental health or when I narrowed it down and looked at specific disorders, disorders like depression and, you guessed it, anxiety.

Regardless of what I typed in the rectangular search box, I would find some scientifically-valid connection between mental health and running or other forms of exercise. Much of the literature explained how, for example," Running increases blood flow, neurotransmitters like serotonin to the brain and thereby diminishing the effects of anxiety, boosting one's mood and providing a sustained, overall sense of well-being." Essentially, running appeared to be a potent form of mother nature's medication.

While I had never been especially athletic, especially in my teen years, I was willing to try anything and everything. All I wanted was my life back, to get back to work, and build a home and family with my children.

This newly acquired knowledge gave me hope and with it, I set out on a running program. As it would turn out, the scientists were right. While my remarkably out-of-shape self found it to be a hellish and gruelling experience at first, I stuck with it. I could feel the thrust of using my anxiety disorder and my dream of being every bit of the good dad my two beautiful kids deserved, as the fuel to propel me forward. "Having my family back is the finish line" became my mantra.

The Beginnings of Recovery
The Miracle that Is Exercise

Armed with a solid mental-health wellness plan and goals to chase, I found that the simple dream of getting back to work and building a meaningful life with my kids was so energizing, I quite literally hit the ground running. As fate would have it, less than three minutes from my parents' home was a beautiful walking and running trail. A railroad track in its former life, it had been torn up and re-purposed for community recreational use.

I loved this area of my hometown. It's mostly level, well-groomed gravel path with lush green trees lining either side, made it a perfect place to bring my fitness goals. I found it very inspiring and overall great for the soul. Its natural beauty accentuated by farmers' fields and views of the mountains in the background, produced a calm within me that made all my troubles feel melted away. Accruing a "runner's high" over time added to my inner peace by allowing me to experience a rare phenomenon in my life, happiness. Oh, the euphoria!

Being immersed in mother nature has a way of making you think of life in a totally different context. If I am anything to go by, it can help redefine your priorities and allow you to not only see the pleasantries of life, but also help you gravitate toward more positive people. What I was experiencing proved to me that life had more value than I had once imagined. It was in these early days with my exercise leg of the journey that I learned to appreciate the beauty of the world that surrounds me. "I need to stop and be present in these moments," I said to myself. Since then, I will often stop what I am doing, breathe deep, taking all the beautiful sounds around me, and feel my mental pain melt away.

I couldn't help but notice that there was something happening to me, inside my mind and in my soul, something amazing, transformative even. And all because I was moving my body like never before.

Just as mental illness had hijacked my brain and thus altered my life to the degree I couldn't work, jogging's power was just as profound, only in the opposite direction. The power that this brand of physical fitness had over me was like nothing I had ever experienced before and, as my body became more and more accustomed to it, my mind was freed to reap all of its euphoric benefits, thus putting the power back into my hands, Finally, I was the captain of my destiny and I told anxiety how things were going to go, not the other way around. "Mother nature really is the best medicine." It was like a prescription to myself.

The multi-sensory inputs that greeted me with every step along the trail, only heightened my experience. The air entering my lungs as I worked hard to time my breathing, melted away the deep sense of dread that comes standard with an anxiety disorder.

The light breeze that I collided with as I moved forward was invigorating and its aftermath provided me with a sustained inner peace that was unmatched by any man-made attempt to reproduce a synthetic version of the same amazing feeling. When I think about the benefits of exercise, I learned that the euphoria that came with it would not be immediate. Quite the contrary. Starting a workout routine is pure hell, but is the hell that is worth the heaven that comes after. "Oh, my god, I can't do this," came flying out of my mouth on several occasions, but once I got used to it, it felt so good and so normal that "Oh my gods" turned into, "Man, I love how I am feeling. My mind is clearer and I can, for the first time in my children's lives, run with them."

And as far as my mental health went, well, if I started to feel weighed down by anxiety or slowed by the dread of depression, I knew to run. "I know how to beat you," I could now say. Looking back, I know without a doubt, that taking up exercise was one of the single greatest choices I've ever made.

Fortunately for me, my move away from medications and towards a more natural and healthier solution ended up being more of a necessity than I had realized. The pharmaceutical treatments my psychiatrist prescribed had little to no effect on my newly-diagnosed mental-health condition. Years later, I would come to learn the reason why. I am an epileptic and the medication I am on for the seizures, renders most antidepressants useless – a sad reality that would have serious consequences later in life. However, because I had found an alternative to medication, it wasn't that big of a concern at the time. "At least I have found an alternative solution. I am glad I can look at all of my options."

Taking on my demons armed with good science and the will to execute what I had learned, I was slowly morphing into a more fit and mentally robust version of myself. It changed me, and as I became physically fitter, the brain fog lifted, my tolerance began to grow, and my world view had begun to change. I was more optimistic and ready to re-emerge amongst the living. Once my body and mind began to love exercise, I began to notice that I was less irritable and so much happier.

But what drove it home for me, when I realized that it was working, was that I was able to keep up with the children. "I used to have to nap all the time," I said to myself, the "me" I often spoke to. "Now I don't need to, and it's great because I can be the active dad I've always wanted to be." Throughout their childhood, I would chase them on the playground, run with him on the beaches and go on an assortment of different adventures with them just about every time we were together.

The Takeaway

So, research was the catalyst that literally transformed my life. Probably the most important lesson for me had been just how difficult it is to embrace an exercise routine and stick to it. Just the sure physical pain and discomfort was bad enough to call it quits. Believe me, I thought about giving up many,

many times. I didn't, and that knowledge made me feel even better. "Science required me to use the logical side of my brain, thus breaking me free from the shackles of my emotions," I acknowledged. "All that I am reading on this is true. It's been a game changer for me."

While the physical conditioning was tough, trying to get a mentally-ill brain going in a healthier direction is like trying to move a full-sized bull out of the middle of the freeway. I was starting in my mid-thirties and at my feet lay two huge bowling balls of obstacles of fear and uncertainty. Not having any idea what my future looked like, often drained what mental reserves I had.

My mental state, a state that could be made so much better because of exercise, was not running at a capacity to get over the hump when it came to getting this exercise plan going. That's when I came up with a phrase that I still live by today: "Because your anxiety doesn't want you to exercise, that's exactly why you should." "I feel tired" is not an excuse for me because I have learned that most of the time, it's mental illness wanting the control. "Netflix and chill? Not today, my friend."

Essentially, I was like a car that wasn't firing on all cylinders. This makes it more difficult for a vehicle to propel itself forward. I was a screwed-up vehicle. Not only was I up against my body's rather rounded and exhausted frame, I had to overcome a brain malfunctioning to debilitation.

A second saying that helped me to climb over both my mind and body was a saying that I preached to others often in my life: "You may have an addiction, a mental illness that makes your healing more difficult, but you have no excuse not to try." So, I followed my own advice, stuck to the plan and let my will to want to live, fuel my determination.

The final result was a much fitter, more mentally-well me and with it, the proudest and most life-altering personal accomplishment of my life. As my fitness journey evolved, I got to know the challenges that come with self-improvement. If someone was to ask me, "Jonathan, what was the most difficult challenge for you while trying on this part of your wellness journey?" I would reply with, "It's the clean-eating part of it, and oh, the initial gruelling weeks at the start of working out."

Today, I have little trouble with the exercise part of my plan, but I still struggle with the diet. I always tell myself, "Slowly change it, John, and that way it won't overwhelm you." My mentally-ill brain already put enough pressure on me, so the last thing I needed was to add pressure that I didn't need.

What could the new and improved me achieve? Maybe almost anything. It would take strength to return to my workplace, but I would find that strength. All I needed was the all-clear from my psychiatrist.

CHAPTER TWELVE

My Triumphant Comeback

"I could feel myself springing to life with an intense, head-to-toe kind of euphoria that rippled through my body in waves."

It was after more than a dozen visits to the '80s-style office of my psychiatrist, that I came with updates on my improvements. Each session proved to me one thing – that I was getting better, so much better in fact that towards the end of our time together, I felt so good, I was asking him, "Can I go back to work now?' My appointments with him became a great way to gauge my recovery. I could tell that each time we spoke, I was feeling a little better. It was a wonderful feeling to know that I was winning the battle. Just before I went back to work, I remember telling him, "I am feeling so much better."

He picked his head up from what must have been my case file and said, "Yes, based on everything, I agree. I must tell you, too, that you are one of my easiest patients."

At least, that's the gist of what I remember! But his statement reaffirmed to me that I was indeed sticking to my philosophical doctrine of "Do whatever it takes to get better." It was in this moment that I began to realize that, yes, if you do put the work in, have clear-cut goals and a plan to get there – and in my case, it was fixing my mental wellness – you can conquer any obstacle that takes you off your life's path.

At the end of our final session, we both rose to our feet, reached across the fake wood-grained-metal desk, and shook hands. If you could "taste" gratefulness, I could just feel my mouth full of it. I said, "Your help has meant so much to me, so much I can't say enough" – or something like that. Once we said our goodbyes, I turned and made my way into the hospital-like hallway and made my way to the elevators. And – which I'm thankful for – I would never be in that hallway or that tiny office again.

As I wandered out the doors of the mental-health clinic, I was met with a semi-cool spring breeze that settled on my face and seemed to find its way into every pore. And like gas to flames, I could feel myself springing to life with an intense, head-to-toe kind of euphoria that rippled through my body in waves, reverberations. It was as though my entire being was celebrating its liberation from mental illness, and it felt so damned physical.

A rarity in my life, this all-encompassing joy. It was so freeing that, for the first time in an exceptionally long time, I felt absolutely no pain. None. Even today I can recall the intensity of what felt like to me, a final victory over this generalized anxiety disorder. I was the gallant knight that finally had slain this beast. By the time I pulled up on the door handle of my truck, I knew that everything was going to be okay. And in that moment, I knew that I would build and achieve my dream of raising my kids and perhaps just as importantly, in the wake of my recovery, I would also make a comeback. The return of John Arenburg.

I recognized that I would still need the help of a mental-health professional. So, I continued to keep regular appointments with my psychologist, working on recognizing anxiety's' triggers and challenging its negative talk. Most importantly, I kept going and was open to whatever she wanted to try. "Stay the course," I said to myself. "Keep working on your mental health so you *know* you can continue to navigate your way through the world when you get back to living within it." My own counselling background knew the techniques and the role of a therapist. Still, I had to keep reminding myself, "John, her role is not to give you advice, but to help you work through your anxiety."

Although the hard work I had taken on to get to this juncture was instrumental in getting me back on a good track, I would be doing myself a disservice if I didn't also credit the fire department for helping me rise above my personal hell. While being off, I found there were three things that got me through each and every day: being a dad, the wonderful help from my boss and the great mental-health professionals, and finally, my very active membership in the fire service.

Being a firefighter was both a lifesaver and a life-stealer for me. In those most turbulent and uncertain years, it did a few things – like providing me with structure, social connection, familiarity and most importantly, a sense of purpose. I am not whole if I am not helping others. Therefore, the department was a beacon of light, shining through the night, that kept this disabled ship from sinking to a depth that would be unrecoverable. Its helping nature kept me afloat every time the pager went off. Without it, I am not sure where I would be today.

The service was a love-hate relationship for me. On one hand, when I walked through those yellow double doors at the back of the station that led me right into the apparatus bay, full of a variety of red and chrome-plated fire trucks, I would feel their meaning. Each one responsible for helping the community countless times. The lingering smell of an old fire scene floating around the station always produced a good feeling. When it greeted my nose, it reminded me that there was nothing else I would rather be doing.

Yet, on the other, my anxiety went from a "three" to a "nine" just in my stepping over the threshold. Later, in my fire-service years, the heavy angst would become more and more dominant. While I had made great progress in my mental health outside of the station, I would slowly die inside every time I entered the realm of the department. Over time, the adrenaline rush of going to a call was replaced by severe anguish, whether I was sitting on the rig, siren blasting with a silent crew on board, focused and ready to do battle with what lay ahead – or trying to let loose and enjoy one of the department's many social functions.

It was as though I was experiencing micro-trauma, if there is such a thing. Near the end, it had culminated into a sort of post-traumatic shit storm. My refusal to prepare for the mental fallout, by simply ignoring it for years and years, meant that it consumed me. Little did I know that these "micro-traumas" would grow so large, like a fully-involved structure fire, they would one by one end my fire-service aspirations.

It's Off to Work I Go

Having the all-clear to return to work from my psychiatrist, I contacted the director and set up several meetings with her so I could get a feel for what my back-to-work plan would look like. In addition to the all-clear, my psychologist suggested, "An ease-back scenario would be best because it would increase your odds of remaining mentally well and on the job."

"Sounds logical," I said.

Armed with this advice, I felt it become my mission while in these meetings. It was vital to ensure I stayed on track. According to her expert advice, "Going back full-throttle right out of the gate almost always ends up in disaster and resulting in more time off."

My director was as supportive of this approach as she had always been. When I presented her with this knowledge, she told me that she would put me anywhere I wanted to go.

When she told me this, I remember feeling almost as euphoric as I had the day I walked out of my psychiatrist's office, out of the mental-health clinic. I felt as if I was a truly valued employee. As a result, it dispelled the notion in my head that somehow this was going to end up being some sort of punitive action. It quelled any anxiety I was experiencing, and it ended up becoming one of the driving forces that made me not only want to come back, but also made me want to stay. That seemed like real growth, an advance that was better than the biggest raise. It sent me a message that being part of her team mattered. Without a doubt, this was one of the most significant contributions to my recovery, just knowing I was valued.

"You are valued, John Arenburg," I swore I could hear around me. "No matter what has happened, what you have thought, what you have done...you have worth."

If it were not for my director's compassionate stance with my situation, I would not be here today. I will always remember her support. Not only did it save my life, it re-ignited my love for my work and made me feel like I owed it to her to do what I had to, to stay mentally well. I have learned that along my route in this life, finding reasons to stay motivated will give you the strength to keep going. Of course, it never hurts to have help and support from others along the way.

Since she left it up to me where I wanted to work, I decided that I needed to minimize all those things that contributed to my illness in the first place. Fortunately for me, I was very aware of my old work area's role in the demise of my once-robust tolerance. The violence, tight quarters and the unimaginable noise, coupled by the ever-present heightened alert brought on by the constant threat of danger, had taken such a toll that I knew that – while I loved that type of clientele – I could never again cope well enough in those conditions to go the emotional distance, not without suffering a similar fate. I also knew somewhere deep inside of me that, regardless of where I ended up in the building, I would not see retirement working for this organization.

"You'll end up in your golden years with something or someone else, John." My constant voice to myself was nothing to be afraid of. It just "was."

Fortunately for me, this long-term care facility had a diverse population. This diversity ranged from the behavioural folks I worked with originally, to heavy-care units where there were people who required assistance with everything from their personal care to eating. The beautiful people living on these two units were for the most part nonverbal and, most importantly, lacked the ability to act out in a physically-violent nature.

That was a great relief to me, and it seemed fitting that I would try making my return on one of these units. Although it was a role filled mostly with female staff members, I decided that perhaps this difference would help me regain my footing. All I knew at the time was that I was willing to do whatever I had to, so long as it was still helping people and not destroying me in the process.

Before I knew it, I found myself walking back through the very same lightweight aluminum-framed doors that six months earlier I had stomped out of and swore that I would never walk through again. Entering the lobby and greeting the rose-coloured stairs and a matching runner up the middle, I recall being there at the foot of them, moments away from my brand new right out-of-the-box work environment. I felt myself freezing. Frozen...All of a sudden, it was as though someone had installed an invisible force-field, preventing me from getting on with it. "What the f – ?" For a few long moments, I resisted the urge to turn and run. I had to remind myself that, while I was entering the same building, the unit I was going to be working on was nothing like the environment I had headed to work in for the best part of eight years.

Despite that fact, I hated the great unknown and made-up scenarios of what I was going to encounter. "What If I'm not good enough?" "Have I made a huge mistake?" "What If I fail?" "As a guy, can I even do this heavy-care thing?" An entire yet invisible avalanche of what-ifs fell on me, weighing me down and preventing me from placing my foot on that first stair tread.

After regaining my composure by using the cognitive behavioural techniques my psychologist was teaching me, I mustered up the courage to make it up the mountainous staircase and down the long hall to the main door of my new work adventure. What my anxiety was asking could happen, but there was an equal chance that none of them would – this is the power of cognitive-behavioural therapy

Walk The Plank, Right Into the Thick of Things

As I stepped on to the unit, I was immediately taken aback by just how much cleaner and more intact the walls and doors were. My old unit was always bearing the brunt of the aggression that was ever-present. I thought "I already like the brighter, calmer atmosphere." Maybe it was the soft yellow paint that blanketed the walls from one end of the unit to the other, or perhaps it was the subdued lighting and the lack of chaotic stimulus. Whatever the case, I could recall feeling my anxiety ease up.

Being an employee at this residential care facility for the best part of ten years, I spent a little time passing through all eight of the units and because of this, I knew right where the office was.

A bit late because of my near meltdown at the main entrance, I walked up to the office to discover that the two sectioned wooden industrial doors were closed. The night-shift nurse was giving a report to a half-dozen staff members all dressed in scrubs, sitting in or moving around inside. I was quietly ushered into the former nurses' station and stood in the corner.

Fuzzy on the intricate details of that day, I would learn that I would be there only for a couple of weeks. After that, I would be transferred to the other heavy-care unit. Nonetheless I was there long enough to fall in love with helping this vulnerable population. What an honour to be one of those charged with the responsibility of caring for those, who, without it, would have not survived. While the work was much more physical and very repetitive, I welcomed the change. Lacking the mental stress and unpredictability of my previous work environment, my mental health kept on an even keel, and I could feel it. "You are stable."

This necessary change reinvigorated my love for my work. In fact, as a way to gauge my newfound contentment and love, I knew it to be true when I once again realized I enjoyed getting out of bed and going to work. No better acid test than that. No dragging of feet, no sick pit of the stomach, just good feelings.

To this day, I still understand just how profound it was to be met with understanding and compassion from my employer. Certainly, they could have chosen a different approach but instead, they gave me everything I needed from them to recover. My director's support was nothing short of amazing. I often think of it as a centrepiece that helped me push back against the mental-health condition that threatened to end it all, literally. How much faith I placed in her hands. In a very real sense, she was the decider of my fate.

The Move

Despite being on the unit for only the two weeks and working only half shifts, I found that it was enough time to get used to the routine and get to know the residents and staff. When the move came, I don't recall being overly upset about it. I think it was mostly because I was still revelling in my return and being proud of my personal and professional accomplishments. Honestly, as long as it wasn't working with aggressive individuals and copious amounts of screaming, I didn't care!

What was good about my two-week warm-up with the first unit was that I could easily take on a similar but different work area. Despite my reclaiming my rightful place over my anxiety disorder, it still lurked in the background. This was especially evident when I landed on this new unit. There it was, yelling at me with all its standard taglines. These one-liners, the ones I experienced when I first entered the building two weeks before, were present the day I made my way down the roughly three-hundred-foot hallway that opened up to a huge day-room and came to a stop at the staff office.

Like my previous unit, it was clean, in great shape and calming. The lights were dim, and the light sky-blue walls made it feel pleasant to be there. In comparison, the people who lived here were remarkably similar in terms of their needs, requiring assistance with every facet of their lives. And like the other unit, it too was more physical, quieter for the most part and almost aggression-free.

There were differences though: this unit had more people living on it, and their care needs were higher and thus more demanding. I remember it well because for the first while, it was physically exhausting and so busy. I can recall fading one day as I was caring for a resident. I said to the charge nurse,

"Look, I really doubt my abilities to be able to go the distance with this particular type of care."

I could see how she was trying to reassure me: "I understand how you feel, John, but you will get used to this kind of workload. A bit overwhelming at first, but you're up to it."

It turned out she was right; I did become accustomed to the hustle and bustle of the unit and spent the remainder of my career working with and caring for some of the most genuine human beings I have ever met. These folks who we were charged to look after were completely dependant on us, almost all of them wheelchair users who had very limited use of their arms or legs. I loved knowing that I was making a difference. Without us, they wouldn't have made it.

"It was a total honour and privilege to be a part of their lives," I find myself thinking a lot. We gave them their Christmases and sang "Happy Birthday!" around uniquely-decorated birthday cakes, and sat at their side when they were sick and dying. For me, it was much like having a second family.

CHAPTER THIRTEEN

My Dreams Realized

"For years I chased the life I was told to chase, and look where it got me. Since then, I have learned that simplicity is bliss."

So far, so good. I felt that warm sensation of being pleased, with how successful I had been reintegrating myself back into the occupation I loved. This second chance at a new beginning was not limited to my work life. Once I had a steady income coming in again, I scraped up every extra dollar and dime for a place I could finally call my own. How good that felt, to have yet another goal to work towards.

Once my bank account was full enough to afford a down payment for a place, I set out to accomplish this goal. I became like a bear on the hunt for food just before winter. I was on a tear to start living again. Within a matter of a weeks after I had the cash I needed for an apartment, I found one!

The landlord and I set up a time for me to view the apartment. This arranged meeting made the prospect of having my own space a potential reality. When it hits, it's almost too much to take in. Excitement, nervousness, a healthy dose of apprehension...When I encounter *that* creature, I often hesitate to take on that new thing, whatever the situation. I would find this always to be the case when I am faced with life-changing moments like this one.

The prospect of starting my life over won the day. As the time to view the apartment grew near, I became so eager and anxious that I went and drove past the place a few times. A newly-constructed, three-storey townhouse, it had an exterior with castle-grey siding, a bay window on the first floor, and two windows closer to the black shingled roof. I assumed that this double window had a bedroom just beyond it. Over the front door to the house was a little triangular overhang, just big enough to completely cover the landing. From the road, this space looked large enough for you to comfortably put a chair out on and watch a summer evening pass you by.

While exciting for me, it also seemed surreal. During one of my trips past the place, it hit me and I thought, "In the very near future, this could be my place." My new life could lie just beyond that standard white, thirty-two-by-eighty front door. What a notion! It only fuelled my excitement, like flame on top of flame, and overriding any fears of what-ifs and "Can I do it?"

Finally, it came, the evening we had agreed to meet. Never one to be late, I arrived early to check out the house exterior up close. I was delighted to see that I had beaten the landlady there. I snuck around to the back of the apartment to find a large deck on the back. A great place to spend my days off, reading or refining the skills I was learning in therapy, playing with the kids or just taking time to soak up the warmth of the sun.

The wait was longer than I anticipated and as a result, I found myself sitting on the front step, getting more anxious as time went by. Inevitably, my curiosity got the best of me, I stood on my feet and peeked through the double-pane glass insert in the main-entrance entryway. Unfortunately, my view was obscured by the early-evening sun and I was not able to see anything past the kitchen area, the first room that lay just on the other side of the door.

Suddenly, I was hit with a wave of panic as I then had the thought of "What if the landlady pulls in and I'm standing here like some burglar, peering in the window making it look like I'm casing the joint?" I felt my face flush, and scurried back to the steps and took a seat once more. Not two minutes later, a gold-coloured Dodge minivan pulled into the driveway. I could barely make out a figure of a person cutting the engine. I finally got a good look when a woman stepped out.

She looked to be around my parents' age, with short greying hair. As she got closer, I could see she had on a pair of those large-lens, rounded-framed glasses apparently from some past fashion era.

From the moment we said our hellos, I sensed that she was one of the always-on-the-go types. Her speech was hurried, with movements to match. I got the strong impression that she was always onto the next task, not necessarily in real life, but in her head.

As she quickly put the key into the lock, I could feel the happy anticipation fill me. I said to myself "Is this actually happening? Am I really doing this?"

When the lock disengaged with a click, she said, "I'm sorry for being late. Not only do I manage these apartments for my boss, I also clean them and get them ready."

"No problem," I said. "It's a beautiful evening so I didn't mind waiting."

As we both went in from the light of the early-evening sunset and into the dimly-lit apartment, I was already impressed by the layout. The kitchen, just as you entered the apartment. Its narrow length, stretching from the front entryway, right to the back door. The rear door leading out to that large patio I had discovered while waiting for her.

Once she had turned on the light to the kitchen, I could see it was a clean-looking, brightly-lit area with eggshell-white cupboards and a white ceiling. The floor was vinyl, fashioned to look like ceramic tile, its neutral grey and light blacks coordinating with the black-covered counter-tops. And it was complete, with more than enough cupboard space. I was relieved to see it housed a standard-size fridge and stove, also that egg-shell white.

Every room in the place was painted in the same colour, a clay-ish shade of grey. Renter-neutral. Immediately off to the left of the kitchen was the living room and dining nook. The nook sat in an alcove made by the bay window I had noticed on one of my many slow drive-bys, trying to catch a glimpse of the place. Both the living room and dining area were dimly lit and adorned with the same dark-brown floating floor.

It technically was a one-bedroom apartment. This singular bedroom was located on the third floor. As we made our way up the stairs and through the door of what could be my new refuge, I was pleased to see it was a bigger-than-average room, with lots of space for the bed I was yet to buy. Though bland, without character, it had a carpeted floor, just a few shades lighter than the walls. I was equally pleased to see the decent-sized walk-in closet to go with it.

"How much is the damage deposit?" I asked.

"Three-hundred twenty-five," she said.

Not bad.

The landlady kept mentioning that the garbage lying around would be gone by the end of the week. "Great," I said. That made me feel they cared about their properties. "I like things clean," I added, "So there will never be an issue there."

She smiled with apparent relief, and then plunged into a story about tenants who trashed the place last time it was rented. "Some people have no respect!" she said with disgust in her voice.

In between showing me the features of the apartment, she began another story on how destructive some people can be, not leaving much airtime for me.

My successfully-contained enthusiasm lessened when it appeared that this one-bedroom apartment wouldn't be able to meet the needs of my family. However, my spirits bounced back as she led me down narrow, walnut-stained basement steps and into the basement. On the bottom step, I was greeted with a huge open carpeted area with the exact same colour scheme as the rest of the place. The only partitioned wall in the entire basement was in the left-hand corner, a small room just large enough to house a washer and dryer and maybe a few things needing storage.

While the layout was less than ideal, my kids were at an age where I could make it work. I knew after seeing the basement that it could easily accommodate them, a thought she echoed when she said, "That corner over there can easily accommodate two beds."

I felt my entire plan coming together. The price was right, the environment clean and modern and best of all, I was mentally well enough to realize my dream, having my family all under the same roof.

By the time we had reached the top of the stairs, then the kitchen, I had made up my mind about renting this narrow condo-like structure that was adjoined to two other units. I said to myself, "Today is the day my kids and I start our new life together." Finally! Psyched by the end of the tour, I said to her, "I love the place. I'll take it."

"That's great!" she said. "I'll need the damage deposit now if you have it."

I happily passed her $325.00 in cash.

With it, I thought, came plenty of opportunities to create memories to last a lifetime – and, I hoped, to let the cohesive nature of family love heal me and all of us, together. That was quite an expectation that came along with this little living unit!

A Brand-New Start

After eagerly signing the rental contract, I returned to my parents' place with "Good news! I've got it – and there's enough room for all of us!" The smiles on their own faces, the happy crinkles around their eyes, told me they were glad for me. Perhaps what made them even happier was knowing they now would have their home back and all to themselves.

"Can't blame you a bit," I said to myself. I also really understood the need to have my own place to call home.

Since the apartment was vacant at the time, all the landlady wanted was a week to give the place a good cleaning. So, after waiting the week, I gathered what remained of my past life, enough to fill the dark-blue minivan I had bought to replace the truck. "Can't run two kids around in a single cab," I said. Besides, it wasn't only outdated, but was ready for the junkyard.

I would need only a few trips to get all my belongings transported to what I could now call "my home." When I left my old life behind, I had decided to minimize the hardship on the kids and leave all our material possessions with their mother. Except for my tools, clothes and personal-to-me-only items, the rest stayed behind. Familiarity is important for small children and I wanted the adjustment to be as smooth as possible for them.

The plus side of having so few possessions was having to make just a few trips to get the job done. The downside was that it made the place look more like a storage locker than a home. I would have to scramble and be inventive when it came to acquiring the things I would need to turn it into a truly livable space. I remember thinking at the time, that the place looked more like a first-year college student's dorm room than a family home. "I need to make this feel warm and inviting, and that's the only thing left to achieve," I told myself.

I didn't even have a bed at the time but did manage to get a fuzzy blue hide-a-bed. This old thing would become my bed for the first few weeks. While it was old and worn, I was and still am grateful for it. Not only did it give me a warm, secure place to sleep, it also served as the centrepiece of my family's life, small in numbers, big on love.

In less than a day, I had everything moved into my, or our, new home.

The One Constant

The only thing left to do was to take the time to say my good-byes to my parents and thank them for all their help and sacrifice. That day, for me, was the definition of bittersweet. I was sad to be moving on from my mom and dad's place and at the same time, looking forward to the first day the kids and I could spend under the same roof as a true family.

I recall the conversation I had just before setting out for the first night all alone. I turned to both of them and said, "You have been the one constant in my life, and though I may not have always expressed how much I appreciate your undying support, I have always, always been grateful for it."

My parents, always short on words during softie-type conversations, simply said, "You're welcome." A quick exchange of hugs, and I was on my way.

I owe a truckload-debt of gratitude to my folks. When I look at their unwavering support since I was a boy, I have come to realize that they were one of only a few positive constants in my life. "Always beyond grateful!" I would tell myself, "for all those moments they picked me up when I fell." Whether it was Dad coming to pull me out of a ditch on a wintry early morning or my mom passing me a dollar or two for coffee when I was broke and down on my luck, they have always done whatever they could to help me.

Besides granting me a safe place to stay while my life was being ravaged by mental illness, there was that moment – when they realized I needed to see a mental-health professional, when I was in middle school. That was the catalyst that made me feel just a little more secure in the world. With such gestures of their love for me, they own most of the credit for helping me succeed in life and to do my best to make the world a better place than when I found it. My appreciation cannot be expressed in human language. All I have to offer is my love, what little support I can give back to them and a heartfelt "thank you."

"Thank you" with tears also goes out to my ever-present sister. Even though she lives nearly two thousand kilometres away, she has always seen me through the darkest times in my life. And despite being so far away, she has always made an impressive effort to come home. The first year I moved into the apartment, she came home for the kids' and my first Christmas together, flying in Christmas Eve and showing up on my doorstep at night.

Her plan? To sleep on that rickety old couch and surprise the kids in the morning. She recognized the significance of this very important moment in our lives and left her only life behind to be part of the magic. Indeed, she awoke to two very surprised and overjoyed kids, happy to see their aunt emerge from where she lay. Her efforts made it feel like a Christmas miracle to them. I must admit, it left me feeling like a kid myself.

"Truly the best sister a brother could ever have – you're amazing!" Just made for a Christmas card, you might say.

To New Beginnings

With the last box pulled out of the van and dropped on the narrow kitchen floor, I felt exhaustion washing over me and my adrenaline-fuelled mood get sucked down a drain. I felt that it was taken out of me more intensely by the mental and physical double-header toll the day had taken on me.

With what felt like the last ounce of strength, I walked over to the hide-a-bed, and pulled up and out on the nylon hook that was designed to pull out the thin-framed and spring-assembled bed part of the sofa. Then, rooting for sheets in every box I had scattered about from kitchen to living room, I found some, and with smiles as well as gargantuan effort, stretched the fitted sheet over the custom-made mattress. Yawning all the while, I knew I was ready to let sleep claim me.

Having the bed all made up and thinking I should fall asleep in no time, I found that the silence of the apartment and excitement of the day shut down everything but my mind and my eyes. Lying on my back, body like lead, and staring at the ceiling, I have to say it was the quietest I've ever experienced to date. So silent, in fact, that it was downright lonely. No cable, no internet, not even a TV. Just me, trying to go to sleep in the living room of a strange place with nothing but my few possessions and cell phone to keep me company.

When morning came, I was greeted by the early morning sun blazing through the uncurtained picture window. Still exhausted, with a head full of gritty cobwebs, I slung my feet over the side of the bed and gave myself a few moments to come around. As the fog began to clear, it once again dawned on me that I was alone and that I was on day one of this brand-new, making-it-on-my own adventure.

As my wits returned, I had little else to do but look around at the chaos I'd created last night. I got up and did my best to try to get a game plan going, and to figure out how to even get started.

But before I could put a plan of action in place, I needed the proper fuel for the job. Coffee, the life blood of millions. Because a coffee pot was still on my to-get list, I had no choice but to go to the local coffee shop for that much-needed boost. Fortunately for me, it was less than a five-minute walk. When I arrived, there were many regulars in line, one after another standing there like zombies waiting at feeding time. I assimilated myself into the queue and slowly moved closer to the counter. Once there, I was greeted by a long-time employee.

"Medium double-double?" she said.

"Yes please," came out in my horrid, deep and unmotivated morning voice.

Once I had gotten my coffee and made for my new home, I was struck – it felt almost like "assaulted" – with a sense of pride when I turned on to my street and my place came into view. It came so suddenly and was so intense, and in it was also a complete and utter sense of perfect well-being. And even though I was not looking forward to the task ahead of me, I somehow knew in that moment that everything would work out. I recall saying to myself, "This is going to be a wonderful, life-changing adventure. This is a new life and finally, I am free to build it so I can work on me and recover."

When I fumbled the key into the lock and unlocked "my" door for the first time and entered, I was again reminded that here I was living without so much as a bed, mattress, bedframe or TV. Nothing. "Yes, minimal living can be great for one's mental health," I'd say to myself. "And yes, that's exactly what I was going for. Still, my man, you still need the essentials" – which, at the time, I was severely lacking.

It took me all of two days to unpack. One would have done the trick, but work took priority. I'd also decided to pace myself simply because otherwise I would quickly run out of things to do. While taking everything out of the boxes, I was busy taking inventory of what I had and what it was I needed. It's hard to make Kraft Dinner without a pot to cook it in, to access the internet without a computer, and to get things set up for the kids without beds for them.

With each item I gave a home to, somewhere in the apartment, a panic set in and grew throughout the day as the reality of my situation became more and more apparent. Now that I was in and had spent all my savings on the four walls that surrounded me, how was I going to afford a washer and dryer, a bed and something as simple as a pot set? "You stupid twit," I said to myself. "Ill-prepared, to put it mildly." I'd been so eager to get my life back on course that I'd made the housing decision in haste. Having run the gamut of emotions – mad, sad, still happy – I at least had a home. "Now what?" I said to myself. "Now what are you going to do?" I was paying child support and my budget was thin as a scraped razor.

It would be a week or so before the kids would come to stay, and I was doing my best to get everything we needed to get our lives on track. The only thought I had that made this reality bearable was the image of their faces. This would have to be enough to get me through, until they came. "Somehow, some way, we are going to make it as the Arenburg Clan," was my mantra.

I could feel the eagerness in my chest – I think the heart had a lot to do with it – of "I can't wait for all of us to get this new chapter underway." I was also saddened and impatient, the typical emotional mix-up. Just knowing we would all soon be together was enough to get me through those long and eerily quiet days and nights. I remember saying, "John, you're a hot mess, keep your cool, it will all work out."

Once every item had been put away, the open-concept nature of the apartment seemed to make the lonely feeling worse. A wide-open space, as nice as it was, made the waiting game excruciating.

On the plus side, I was still very physically active, and I was still running a lot. "Thank you again," I said to myself, for turning to exercise. Not only was I getting even more fit with every run, I was putting my energy into feeling better about being the single occupant of a large, barely-furnished townhouse. Getting out into nature was better than staring at empty walls and eggshell-white ceilings. I also was happy to be working twelve-hour shifts, three days a week and sometimes more. Working these long hours was perfect. It killed entire days, living that minimalist life – reporting for work at seven in the morning and working until seven in the evening saved my sanity. I basically got up, went to work, came home, and went to bed.

The other benefit was that it occupied my time so I wouldn't be consumed by missing the kids, or my worries around where I was going to get a bed for myself and for them. Starting over costs big bucks when the majority of what you need is big-ticket items. So naturally, thinking about the sheer number of things I had to buy was overwhelming. With all that, work was a welcome reprieve.

Human Kindness to the Rescue

Every time I graced the threshold of my apartment, I was reminded of just how much I needed in order to actually start living. Things also really hit home once I calculated my newly-acquired debt load. Twenty to forty dollars every two weeks and being bankrupt wasn't going to make getting appliances and the like easy. Rather, they were looking unobtainable. There it was, my reality staring back at me, in black and white. I remember saying "Well, now, what the hell ya gonna do?"

Gutted by my sliced-thin budget, I also thought, "How in the hell can I pull this off?" With that budget, my kids and I would have to share the hide-a-bed three ways. I needed so many big-ticket items, necessities that were going to be out of my financial reach. What a mess.

Sickened by this overwhelming, "What am I going to do?" moment for the first time in an exceptionally long time, I had no idea. I had come so far, worked so hard, and here I was, broke, was going to be living my life alone half the time – and convinced that this environment was not going to allow me to be the father I had always dreamed of being. Broke! The world just seemed to have it in for me.

My pride had been a roadblock for me before, and this instance was no exception. Life's brutal sting forced me to swallow that pride and helped me to understand that I had to make this work. Like the firefighter at the door, regardless of circumstance, fire, near-death, there was no turning back.

Once again, my children fuelled my desire to do what I had to do. This whole situation may have hindered my ability to be the dad I wanted to be, but that didn't mean I shouldn't try. Giving up wasn't an option and never once crossed my mind. "All right, John, into problem-solver mode you go. And you've got to be both brave and creative."

In desperation, or what I'd prefer to call "creative problem solving," I turned to Facebook for help. With a virtual hat in hand, I summoned the courage to ask people "Do you have any large household items you're trying to get rid of? If so, I'll gladly take it off your hands. The only catch? It has to be free." Only minutes after hitting the "post" button, I heard a voice in my head call me a failure. This sentence unleashed the power of my anxiety disorder, and it didn't play nice.

I envisioned people calling me a "bum" and a "loser," a "mooch" and a "freeloader," all the things I was petrified of being. Not even a run could tame the anxious beast. I was so scared of what I might find in the way of responses that I was too overwhelmed to check. "I have to delete that post – I'm pathetic."

A sleepless night and a day later, I finally felt brave enough to open the app to see if anyone had responded. Clicking away with my anxiety at a near nine, what I discovered is that once again, anxiety had lied to me, as is always the case, every single time. What I saw in the comment sections, right before me in black and white, was not ridicule nor shaming, but rather friends stepping up coming to my rescue.

I sat, staring at my phone's tiny screen in disbelief. I could hardly believe what I was reading. So many people had answered my pleas, so many were ready, willing and able to help. With offers of everything from toasters to pots and pans, to beds for the kids. I was so moved by this outpouring of generosity, tears welled up in my eyes. In an instant, the anxiety was stamped out like a small fire. My irrational expectation of what I thought was going to happen was replaced with overwhelming joy. In these moments of absolute despair, my faith in humanity was restored.

As one who has been a helper all his life, I wasn't used to help being reciprocated. In fact, I really felt deep down that I wasn't worthy enough to accept the kindness being thrown my way. Fortunately, I knew I had to toss that aside and embrace it. At this fork in the road, I had two choices – to get over myself and accept the help I desperately needed, or hold onto this notion of being not deserving of their generosity and lose the very life I had been working so hard to build. "Really, what choice do you have?"

That one post on Facebook started an avalanche of support. With nothing but the kindness of others, I was able to furnish my entire apartment. The outpouring of help gave me much more than I'd asked for. Most of these extra things that people gifted, I would never have been able to afford on my own. A washer and dryer, a TV and even a game console, pots and pans, coffee makers, cups, plates, and cutlery. Simply amazing. Seeing the replies, like, "John, I have a hide-a-bed." And another one: "We have a ton of stuff in our barn that our son had for his first place, you are welcome to it." These were but a few of the offers I had received. What's more, people even loaded up their trucks and dropped it off to me.

The takeaway? There's real power in accepting generosity into one's life. People are often all too happy to lend a hand, like me. Since those days, I have developed a few rules. I committed to being kind to those who help me, do what I can to pay it forward and understand that support from others makes the world a better place. "I am so lucky to have such wonderful people in my life."

The Beauty of Friends and Family

One thing that this generosity highlighted for me was just how down I was about everything at the time. While my healing journey had brought me a long way, and out of a self-destructive mindset, nothing provided me with more clarity and direction than this demonstration of human kindness. It's easy, especially when one has a mental illness, to see others in a negative lens because one is always on guard for it. I was no exception. It's as if it came as second nature to find fault with everyone.

But this, this new revelation was like a breath of fresh air, a feeling so wonderful that I was delighted to be wrong. This feeling was only reinforced when my friends and family came to my rescue. Mom and Dad, being the ever-consistent and positive support in my life, showed up on my doorstep one evening with a twin-sized mattress – "John? We thought you could use this!" – they had bought for me so I could finally claim the bedroom I wasn't able to sleep in. That gesture was huge – bigger than the mattress measurements. It gave me back a sense of normalcy and reminded me that my parents were always willing to help in any way they could.

With each act of unrequited kindness, my mental health saw an ever-steady improvement; making these gestures life-altering, life-transforming. They were huge! When my life hit rough seas that surely would have sunk me, the good will of my family and friends was lighthouse, life preserver, rescuer and more.

This fact was made even more evident by the above-and-beyond acts of a fellow firefighter whom I think of as more of a brother than a friend. Seemingly from two different worlds but bonded together through similar life experiences, we had become close as our years of service together moved on. A jack-of-all-trades kind of guy with an overwhelming need to always keep busy, he worked day and night and when he wasn't trying to provide for his large family, he was always helping others. I remember him randomly popping through my door, a jug of milk in one hand and a carton of eggs in the other, He looked at me and said, "As long as you have eggs, you have a meal," turned around without saying another word, and left. He is all about the random acts of kindness.

If you have ever watched the show *Duck Dynasty*, then you can picture my colleague in the flesh: a long, dark, unkempt beard covered his face, and his garb reflected his hands-on work ethic, always well-worn and streaked with the stains of his accomplishments.

And, despite being a little rough around the edges temperament-wise, he is without a doubt the most generous human being outside of my family I have ever met. I would come to know it well as I struggled to make a go of my new life and well beyond.

There are moments in life that we never forget. The moments that inspire us, that make us a better person and that when thought of, ease our suffering. One such moment was carved out in my memory and in my heart when my non-blood-related brother saved me from a potentially isolating prospect.

As fate would have it, not long after the outpouring of support from people who helped to get me on my feet, I discovered that my van's frame was so rotten that it was too expensive to repair. This discovery was devastating and its implications huge. Sure, I could make arrangements to go back and forth from work, and the inconvenience that created was the least of my issues.

What was most problematic was its implications for my family. The kids would need to go to school, doctor appointments and play-dates with their friends – and what of little family trips and relaxing drives? Surely in this circumstance there really was no way around it. I would have to do my best with what I had, support from others and my own two feet.

"So, this fate has been decided for me," I grumbled to myself. "Now what the hell is an alternative to make this work?"

One mid-morning I was startled by the ring tone as it shattered the silent air. On the other end was my friend, my "brother." I frowned – with surprise. He very rarely called. After a short and to-the-point intro, he said, "Do you want to buy a car?"

"I don't have the money," I said.

He repeated the question, more impatiently.

"Yes, man, but I haven't got the money."

Eventually it came out. He had come across an old Chevy Malibu for sale while doing one of many independent small jobs he was known for.

Then he said, "Look, John, I'll pay for it. You can pay me back later, whenever."

It's as if I was driven to do it. I reluctantly said yes to his offer. Hanging up the phone, I stood, speechless and frozen. I couldn't believe this man, a father of five and a single-income earner, would do that for me. Even now, it's a job to articulate just how much his act of kindness meant and still means to me today.

What I didn't know at the time was that when he negotiated the price, the owner would not go as low as my friend could afford. So, in what must be the ultimate act of kindness, unlike anything I have ever been given, he then offered to work the remaining balance off for free. Fortunately for me, the seller agreed to the terms laid before him and in only a few days, one golden-coloured '97 Chevy was sitting in my driveway.

My friend's help came at a time when I needed it most. I still can't believe it! Because of his above-and-beyond support, I felt the accumulated stress and triggered anxiety disorder held at bay. Thanks to him, my self-worth was at an all-time high and with it, my negative outlook was taken down a level or two. I was determined to pay back every dime regardless of how long it took, and vowed that our friendship would be built upon mutual respect and support.

Amazingly, he who I considered my brother didn't stop there. I often found his bearded face in the window of my door, grinning above an unsolicited arm-load of milk and eggs. Even when something needed fixing, he was there. Didn't matter if it was my car in need of repair or my washing machine on the fritz, he was my life-saver on many occasions.

In return, my experience in helping others with their emotional and psychological needs was my strongest asset and so, I made myself available to him, always, to help him through his tougher, trying times. Even to this day, I would drop everything I was doing to help him with whatever he needed. We are brothers.

Although his generosity seemed to know no bounds, there were others throughout this time period in my life, who helped me so much. From another friend who crawled under the hood of one of my cars I bought a few years later, spending four hours in the sun to fix it – to people offering everything from food to emotional support and anything in between.

To learn is to grow and in those uncertain days, I grew in ways that I never thought I could. Since then, I have never lost faith in humanity. If anything, it has strengthened my desire to help others in a pay-it-forward fashion.

Now when anxiety takes me down the long road of negative thought, I use these beautiful moments in my life to ground myself and by doing so, I feel the fog lift and with it, my spirit brighten. Perhaps the greatest gift I took away from it all was the gift of being kinder. Kindness is a mental-illness healer, without question.

It's amazing how the acts of others can bring out and cultivate your authentic self. In my case, it helped me learn that we all need help along our journey, all of us. Since then, I have tried to treat all of humanity with the same level of caring and understanding I've been given, and that surely, we all deserve.

We Are Family… Finally!

Thanks to the overwhelming acts of kindness of people, and some I didn't even know, my apartment went from looking like an abandoned, rundown space with only a few items, to a just about fully-furnished residence, with the feeling of home. Although things didn't quite go how I envisioned they would when I stepped out on my own, I was no stranger to life's more inconvenient, out of-my-control moments. Therefore, I accepted that my life had led me down a road that I never intended to venture on.

Still, when I think back on this time, I have come to understand that, as long as you work hard to better yourself and treat others well, things can work out well.

It had now come together in a way that let me enjoy my new family dynamic: just me, my son and my daughter. It was an existence full of joy but at the same time I knew that the transition for them wouldn't be easy. I chose to do it in stages if necessary so they could get used to the changes over time. My young fella, around eight at the time, appeared as excited as I was. My daughter, on the other hand, was two when I left. With the exception of her coming over for the day while I was living with Mom and Dad, I'm sad to say I didn't see her that much. I had the truck at that time when she was young, and it was one I couldn't really take her in – so old I didn't feel it was safe.

During the years between moving out of the family home and moving into this new space, I had little opportunity to get to know her on a level that all daddies should know their little girls. It's a reality I regret, even to this day. While I make no excuses for how things played out between her and me, by the time she came along I was at the peak of my mental-illness battle. I had to struggle to lift my head out of bed, let alone be fully attentive to the cultivation of a father/daughter relationship.

When I think back on it now, it fills my heart with sadness, as I envision her beautiful little self, with that adventurous spirit and sometimes-cranky disposition, those blue eyes with a touch of green in the middle. I feel a sting of regret that only one who wanted to be a fully-present and functioning dad would feel. Those days we will never get back. Because of these lost years, I will always feel an emptiness, a void that should have been filled with diaper changes, hugs and little toddler adventures.

Thanks to this new living environment, our new family had a place to call home and with it, my daughter and I would forge a dad and daughter relationship that I had always dreamed of. In fact, our bond had become so strong, it exceeded everything I had dreamed it would bloom into.

While I could never make up for the lost time, her being so young was as much a blessing as it was a heartache. My gal, who I effectively call "kid," would come to rely on me as her go-to person for her own little anxiety-ridden heart, a battle I still stand fighting with her to this day. Our relationship may have had a rough start, but now? Now I will spend the rest of my days helping her through her toughest battles.

Because of the age difference between my son and daughter, my son being the oldest, we had more years in which to cultivate a relationship. He was known mostly to me as "boy," and our dad and the lad relationship grew stronger even after I landed at my parents.' Because he was older, I felt safer taking him for drives in my old beater and going on adventures. It became a thing for us to drive around in search of dead-ends, a long-lasting memory we still revisit today. "Boy! Want to go for a drive and find some dead-end roads?" I was always greeted with an enthusiastic "Yeah!"

A fella with a lovely kind heart from the very beginning of his life, he has always had a way of making you feel better. It seemed as if, like me, he just innately knew how to help. Those deep blue eyes of his could shine like stars, even more so when he was happy, and it was enough to spark a smile on anyone's face.

His tendency to be kind and helpful wasn't the only thing he acquired as a baby. His love for all things cars blossomed at this time too. Much to his mother's and my disappointment, his first word wasn't "Mom" or "Dad" – it was "Car." Our secret hope that at least one of us would be his first word didn't become too painful; rather, we were delighted at the fact it was somewhat non-traditional and very unexpected. It became a fun conversation piece.

I couldn't tell you definitively where he had picked up this passion, but I do know that ever since it rolled off that beautiful blond-headed little boy's tongue, it has become his one and only passion. Even now, many years later, his dream has not wavered, not even an inch. Rather, it has intensified to the degree where he is working on becoming a mechanic.

Who Knew That Being Broke Could Be Beautiful?

As we gently eased into our new lives together and the stress and anxiety were alleviated with time, we would learn some great lessons together, while barely holding on financially and having some monumentally tough and stressful days. I would eventually find peace and come to terms with the situation we were in.

In fact, I wouldn't change my financial situation for anything in the world. Even if I could somehow turn back time, I would still choose to live "impoverished." Sound outlandish? Through this harrowing process, I not only learned what it meant to be a good human, but it helped teach me to be a great dad. Normally, being well-off provides a human with a whole multitude of options, options like fancy houses, cars and the latest tech gadgets.

Being broke gave me the one thing all the money in the world cannot provide – the gift of time, and the freedom to build memories with those I love. "All I want is to focus on my kids," was almost like a song to me.

Living a precarious lifestyle forced me to spend time with my children, good quality time. But it did more than that for us. It allowed us to explore opportunities we likely never would have had time to take together. In a position where I had to be nothing but creative, I had to plan trips that were little- to no-cost for us. We would explore free museums, reading days at the library and riding our bikes or finding some beautiful walking trails.

But out of all the memories that have been seared into my mind from those days, are the ones that were created on our Friday-night movie nights. Having only an eighty-dollar DVD player and an old 32-inch tube style television, we would gather on the hide-a-bed, eat our treats, and watch the latest kid movies. Huddled together, snuggling and falling asleep often before the movie was even over created a warm, loving feeling that will stay with me forever. I remember going through a Scooby-Doo phase, I started to do the Scooby-Doo laugh, which made us all laugh. They would both holler, "Do it again!" Before our Friday evenings on the couch, I had no idea just how many Scooby-Doo movies there were, so many in fact, we would all find ourselves saying, "I would have gotten away with it too, if it weren't for those meddling kids." A line in every movie when the bad guy was finally caught.

The takeaway for me here was this: this type of bonding, especially where our relationships had been so strained and fragmented for so long, was meaningful beyond measure. Nothing comes close to that emotional connection we were able to cultivate.

As far as I'm concerned, no trip to Disneyland, no fancy vacation could possibly outmatch the growing and good times we did together as a brand new, three-person family.

What I find amazing is that my decision to leave because of my mental health ended up having the outcome I was so hopeful for. I would be able to manage my life within the tolerances that were built in and custom-made for me. And because I was now paying attention to my true authentic self, my family thrived and did so, well beyond my wildest dreams. "I can't believe I am doing it, I'm beating this mental-illness thing and we are growing together, as a family." I could say that and believe it.

Like any good parent, all I wanted was the best for my children. Being mentally ill myself, I was desperate to ensure that these two beautiful little human beings would grow up to have relatively stable mental health. While I understand that there are many factors that go into developing a mental illness, I was determined to do my best, in a day-by-day, every-moment effort to ensure that they did not end up in my shoes.

I tried to accomplish this by teaching them resilience and providing them with a good moral base on which to conduct themselves. I would often say to them, "It's okay to cry if you were hurt, or to be upset or angry, but we must work on a plan to move past what is causing our problem and learn from it."

Respect for others and people's property was something I absolutely needed them to have. More important than that, however, I needed to teach them to respect themselves. I theorized that if they were polite, moral and worked hard, everything else would fall into place – things like their academics, the pursuit of their dreams and the confidence to achieve whatever it is they wanted to achieve. Every time we were at a store I would say "Please say thank you," to the nice person behind the counter. If they did not, I was insistent that they did.

Finally, my lifelong struggle would become my strongest asset when it came to raising my kids. What I once thought was so destructive, so crippling that there was no way it would be proved to be any benefit whatsoever, I slowly began to see as accumulated wisdom. Having kids provided me with the opportunity to apply that wisdom to help them become well-adjusted, productive members of our society. Even to this day, I am grateful for the long mental-illness journey I have been on. Now that my children are older, I am starting to see the fruits of my labour. Both are passionate and kind, self-confident and helpful people who come to me, open and honest with me whenever life becomes a challenge. Today, my young fellow has no hesitation whatsoever to correct me when I'm not being as polite as I should be. "Dad, they're only trying to do their job. They're not purposely trying to make you angry, so why can't you be polite?"

My daughter will say something similar. She is in cheerleading and the confidence that she displays there has been used to build her confidence in other areas. "You work so hard...we can tell it's paying off, you're such a strong athlete. Your hard work and determination can move mountains for you in any profession you choose to get into." Now, my focus is on teaching them the importance of showing initiative.

My son recently came to me and told me, "Dad, I applied for a job at Walmart." From there, I try to coach him and help with things like interview preparation.

Being their dad, I often consider, is the one thing in my entire life I got right. We have learned so much from one another and we all cherish the relationships we have been able to forge. Such a beautiful thing to go through.

On my quest to be a better dad, I always did my best to impart my wisdom upon them. I also listened when they had a concern, stopping what I was doing to help them through things that were troubling them. But perhaps most importantly, I had taught them that it was okay to communicate with me. "I may be your dad, but I'm human and will make mistakes. Please, let me know if I am doing something that you find hurtful or bothers you."

By giving them permission to express how they feel, we grew closer as a family, built a stronger rapport and learned one another's communication styles. My son found communicating verbally so much easier than my daughter. So, when something was bothering her, we sat down and drew pictures of what it was she needed to discuss. Today, they can come to me to discuss anything they need to. I credit their ability to come talk to me with this approach. Not everything has to be a punishment, a redirection or "Let's wait till later, I'm busy."

Often, I would hear "Dad, can we talk"? followed by "When you told me I couldn't go to my friend's house, it made me angry." I taught them the power of communication and they in turn, made me a better person. While not perfect, I learned to be more patient and less punitive when punishment wasn't really appropriate. Essentially, we all grew together.

While building a rapport with my children had many benefits, it has helped them work through their anxieties and made them more receptive to seeking out external help when they need it. My daughter is a very anxious young lady, but she is able to acknowledge that and is willing to accept any help offered. "Your mother and I will help you find the help you need," I say to her. "You just need to tell us what is going on."

CHAPTER FOURTEEN

My New Life, Definitely Not a Fairy Tale

"Sure enough, a crash was exactly where I was heading. This impending danger could have been prevented had I maintained a professional relationship with my therapist."

This time in my life was without question the most mentally pain-free and enjoyable part of all my years to date – just my kids and me, running around on our low-cost adventures. Even though I was able to quell the chronic worry and low-intensity, trauma-related troubles that had plagued me for so long, I was far from cured. But at the time, I was absolutely convinced I could permanently fight my way out of mental illness's grip.

Despite having my mind made up that I would somehow beat mental illness, and while it's true that at the time I felt more liberated than ever before, the voice of my mental-health condition was always attempting to seduce me back into its chaos, a kind of ugly siren call that could be disguised.

Unknown to me, what I was successful at was not beating mental illness but rather, managing it well. Because this was the first time in my life that I declared all-out war on what it was that mentally ailed me, I failed to understand that this particular type of battle is ongoing. Permanent.

In fact, I was so convinced I had defeated my demons, I had stopped going to counselling. I would suffer the consequences as a result of that decision. In retrospect I should have seen the disaster that was slowly unfolding inside of me. Maybe I didn't want to believe it...?

What I had been successful at was putting distance between myself and my severe anxiety, and had done it so successfully that the anxious voice was but a holler off in the distance. Whereas before, mental illness walked alongside me and was constantly conjuring up worst-case scenarios in my ear. While I knew it never went away, its voice had so little power that I stopped paying attention. That was a colossal mistake, and one that I would pay dearly for as time went on.

My Choices – a Double-Edged Sword

It's funny, you know – one seemingly simple misstep can lead you right back down the road that you had done everything in your power to avoid. In my case, just as I was learning to fly the plane that was my life, straight and true, I underestimated my experience and let go of the controls. I had accumulated skill sets to keep the mental pain at bay, but I was not well-versed on how to prepare for an impending mental emergency.

Because I wasn't aware at that time that when it comes to mental health, there's always the possibility of a crash, I pushed on, oblivious. Mental-health conditions, as it turns out, don't come with an auto-pilot feature. There is no way one can simply cruise through it. My heartbreaking lesson? When you crash, you crash hard. And as if that wasn't devastating enough, it's near impossible to assess just how much damage I inflicted.

Mistaking my progress as a "cure" had slowly melted away any resilience I had accumulated, and dulled the effectiveness of my coping tools. This weakening allowed anxiety to once again overcome me. A few years into my new work placement, the noise once again became insufferable and the busy-ness of the environment overwhelming. I found myself becoming increasingly more agitated, negative, and less and less capable of working. The consequences? The increase of more and more sick time. "I need to be alone, I need quiet." For me the regression was most evident when dealing with my children. I became short and quick to react at any little noise or deviation from the norm. "Be quiet!" became more and more common.

Sure enough, a crash was exactly where I was heading. This impending danger could have been prevented had I maintained a professional relationship with my therapist. Not doing so, set me on a collision course with PTSD,

I am now more certain of that than ever. The best way I can describe it is when someone with mental illness who needs medication to feel better, starts to feel better, and so they stop taking the medication. For people with mental illness who are stable on pharmaceuticals, discontinuing them oftentimes ends up in disaster. This was what it was like for me when I stopped going to therapy.

Hardly noticeable at first, the voice that had ruled me for so long started to make a slow but gradual comeback. I would come to learn that my decision to abandon therapy was a huge mistake. Going on a consistent basis was a fantastic management tool for me, and got me back to work with its abundance of coping strategies. "John, you're losing it again...what's going on? You are still running and eating well...why are you slipping?" I kept saying to myself.

Having picked up strength, the voice of my disorder grew louder and louder. It now had the momentum it needed to pick up speed and before I was even aware of it, it was once again at my ear, controlling and taking me apart from the inside out. I began to notice its grip on me not only by what it was doing to me inside, but what was happening, or should I say not happening, externally. For example, my desire to have a clean home began to take a dip, and the heavier I felt, the less time I spent with even those closest to me. These are things that I now recognize when I start to slip into a depressive episode, for example.

One of the first things I find mental illness does is strip away your positivity. Over the years, following getting back to work, I would become more and more negative. It's as though it's wired to detect every unpleasant thing that goes on. While there are many things in my workplace that needed improvement, I began to focus on every little thing and pick them apart until it consumed any happiness at work I had reconnected with when I'd returned. It feels as though anxiety is hell-bent on destroying the person it has power over: in this case, me.

Work wasn't the only aspect of my life overwhelming to the degree where my ability to ward off my demons was compromised. The fire service was taking its toll, sucking the mental stability out of me.

The death, the destruction and the politics all chipped away at my well-being. It was like being in a malfunctioning elevator, taking me back to the basement floor, and right back to square one of my mental-wellness journey. I would eventually come to find out that what had accumulated in my first half of my fire-service career, never fully dissipated. When the negativity and anxious disposition became too strong to ignore, I knew that I had never really truly dealt with the traumatic events I had been exposed to. Both at work and in the fire service.

I am convinced now, more than ever, that it was at this time period in my life that the atrocities of working in both long-term care and the fire service came together. Like allies, the two of them wore me down by their nonstop potential and actual acts of death in danger.

Now, the question that often arises in my head is: why didn't I see this as I was going through it? How could I not see that anxiety had once again dismantled any semblance of normalcy? The answers were and continue to be somewhat elusive.

I spent a lot of time evaluating just how much damage was done by being a firefighter. I know now just how significant a role it played in altering my life forever. I can only describe it as monumental. My years in the Department have left me lost in a sea of uncertainty. Today, I remain on workers' compensation, my progress halted by the nightmares and the "startle responses" that come standard with post-traumatic stress disorder. It seems as though my years in the service will leave me forever broken. "I can't handle the outside world," is something I've often said to myself, even as I try to do it.

While I wasn't fully conscious of it in those days, over time I began to understand that this constant heavy burden coursing through every fibre of my being, must have something to do with all the death and destruction I was frequently exposed to. The standard narrative didn't help matters either – mainly, that of we "man up" and we don't talk about what we've seen, how we feel or what needs to be done to make it better.

Because I had a love for working in both long-term care and volunteering as a firefighter, the last thing I ever wanted to do was give them up. And as mental illness slowly darkened my days, I often wondered: if I had stuck to one or the other, would everything have turned out fine? While I have my suspicions that I still would have ended up post-traumatic, in reality I will never know.

What I do know is that when you combine two professions that deal with nothing but chaos and death, there is a very good possibility the PTSD will get you in the end. For me, it was a combination of these two jobs that caused me to have an "aha!" moment. After seeing almost ten people pass away in under two years while at work, I started to correlate the numbness and disassociation. The feeling of disconnect and the feeling of being outside of my own body when one is traumatized – the brain does all it can to protect itself. Feeling outside of your body really means you're attempting to detach yourself from the grievous scenario in front of you. Because I felt these symptoms for the best part of two decades, I gradually began to believe that what I was experiencing might in fact be post-traumatic stress disorder.

I even went so far as to wonder if the generalized anxiety disorder I was diagnosed with so many years ago, was actually a secondary diagnosis. Maybe my near-constant angst was being fuelled by my repetitive traumatic experiences? Whatever the case, I gradually started to understand that this could be the case. The question I had to answer was, "What do I have to do to ensure I won't become consumed by what's boiling up from deep within me?"

I had arrived at the conclusion that I somehow was magically healed by my hard work and dedication to fixing myself and as a result, I didn't require any more therapy. While I now know that my hard work and dedication is in fact a lifelong process, my ignorance at the time became the catalyst that would spin my life out of control and see me not only battle PTSD and anxiety, but go toe-to-toe with major depressive disorder. Personally, I feel like depression has always taken up residence within the very core of me. I never once stopped to consider that it was there. Of course, it makes sense now – the sometimes-week-long sabbaticals in the darkness, just lying in bed without the energy to lift my head. The low affect and the chronic exhaustion have been there for a very long time. For many of those years, my irrational worry was so strong it must have blanketed the depressive symptoms. Either that or I had misinterpreted all the factors that were contributing to my illness.

Never Underestimate What Needs to Be Done...No Matter What!

As with carbon-monoxide accumulation, I was slowly being poisoned. There was my unwillingness to continue the healing process through psychotherapy, but also my denial forced me to slug away in an environment that I eventually understood I should have never walked back into. My workplace became a vessel of torment. Throughout my tenure on the unit, the clientele began to change, as those with high needs began to pass away, and people who were more ambulatory, loud and aggressive began to take up residence there.

The changes that were taking place were re-traumatizing me. I felt as though the environment that had once destroyed me, the one I worked in for eight years, had followed me. "Are they trying to drive me crazy?" I remember asking some of my co-workers – referring of course to the management.

In the last two years, I knew, I was barely keeping my head above the traumatic waters, and deep down I knew that my days in long-term care were numbered. Every day I worked, I awoke with a headache, I often trembled at the thought of throwing myself into that war zone I worked in. Eventually, this numbness and anxiety became a permanent fixture, no matter where I went. Whether I was standing over a deceased person in the middle of the 3:00 a.m. moonlight or stepping onto the unit at 7:00 a.m. in the morning, I felt the unrelenting heavy pain and detachment that I came to call "survival mode." I have to work so I needed to embrace the detachment I was feeling. I fully believed that this would provide me with enough protection to keep working. I have always loved working.

As if being in a semi-shutdown state weren't enough, those male voices, the ones in my head that I had effectively beaten back as a younger man, came back with a vengeance, "Man up, there are worse things that can happen," etc.

Even though I knew in my heart that I could no longer mentally handle working in long-term care because I was getting too sick to continue, I did so anyway. Because I knew it, I grew increasingly more angry and resentful. "I hate this place...I have to keep struggling along, it's killing my mental health slowly, I feel trapped!" I thought and spoke in "rushes" like that.

But I had two little kids and by this time a new loving and supportive partner (who I'd met online) to think about.

My new partner was a pure sweetheart to her core. A lover of science, working as a research assistant, she would excitedly tell me about what project or process she was working on. In her downtime, she loved to be creative, with crocheting and cooking her favourite activities. Was this the factor that kept me going during this decline in my health? Always at the ready for a hug and some kind, reassuring words, she made me feel as though I could get through anything.

She was an-ever constant force in my life with its ups and downs. I always felt more at ease every time I came home to greet her, with that long hair – dyed purple, pink and blue – and that beautiful beacon of a smile that made everything so much more bearable.

But in spite of her love and support, I was at a point where I knew in my heart that my days of unfettered mental health were numbered. Something had to give if I was to have any chance of surviving with any sense of normality left. So, one of my long-time helping endeavours had to go. When it comes down to your living or being a volunteer firefighter, the choice is simple, but still not easy to arrive at. I chose my living.

So, I had made up my mind that in order to save myself, I would have to resign from the fire department. I held in just long enough to get my veteran status. This would entitle me to still go to functions and have access to the hall. Holding out gave me the perfect excuse to get the hell out of there while at the same time not having to explain why I was really leaving. I recall telling many of my colleagues, "If I don't make Lieutenant this year, I have my 15 years in, so I will resign."

The prospect of being open and honest as to why I was really bringing my years of service to a conclusion, made me tremble, almost pass out from it. I envisioned being ridiculed and minimized if I opened up and said "Sorry, guys, Chief, I am too sick to carry on." But I remember thinking, "They don't have to know the truth."

I was practically a ghost for the last year I was there. Every time a call came across the little black pager I wore on my pocket or belt, I was grabbed and caged by fear, a fear I could not overcome. I loathed the feeling of having my perceived weakness overcome me. I was scared to death of what my fellow firefighters would think of me, especially those who I had forged close ties with. It was like a tsunami of anxiety that just kept going., All I knew was that I needed a way out that didn't appear cowardly to my colleagues. Really, the only one I had to be loyal to was myself and those who loved and supported me. It was time to stop trying to save others and start trying to save myself. I am grateful that I knew this.

What really led right to the resignation, was this ever-present thought in my head that said; "You're falling apart and you know it. If you get out now, what are the odds of you seeing another deceased person, at least in the streets?" This repetitive notion was what finally gave me the courage to make this "the ending" at my firehouse.

"And since you already work in long-term care," I said to myself, "Leaving the department will cut to the odds to almost nothing, of my involvement with the deceased. All I want at this point is to be a civilian, all I want is peace."

My mind made up and my heart feeling empty, I summoned the courage to turn in my pager and the rest of my gear. "That's it. Done. Finished. No more badge." Amazed in a way that I was able to actually go through with it, I took one last look behind me as I walked out the rear doors and away from something that was so much a part of my life. It will always be integrated with my heart and be forever embedded in my soul. I have entered the building only a handful of times since. To this day, I would love nothing more than to answer the call of the fire siren, but I know that will never again be.

When night fell, I tried to close my eyes, but sleep eluded me as I tortured myself over second-guessing the decision that I had made. "Did you act too hastily?" "Will you regret it?" "Is it better to try and tough it out?" Ultimately though, I would always conclude that I did the right thing because there was absolutely no way I would have been able to continue, not with work on top of it.

For months afterwards, I had vivid dreams and nightmares about the department. The visions were a mix of interacting with the members, and gruesome scenes of car accidents and fires. It was as though my mind refused to believe that the choice I made to get out was a permanent one. "Not so fast, buddy!" it said. "Too much to remember! Gotta re-live it!" Maybe the innate helper in me just didn't want to let go.

I recall it taking forever for the firefighter in me to stop mentally answering fire alarms. The old fire siren mounted on top of the grey, stone-like brick work that ran around the entire bottom three feet of the structure and red corrugated, lightweight sheet metal that covered the rest of the fire hall, wailed its ghostly howl indicating a call had come in to answer. And I would charge to life full of both adrenaline and regret for the decision I made. While this feeling would never leave and still resides within me today, it has dwindled into what would be the equivalent of a single heartbeat in its intensity.

Finally, I am more integrated into civilian life than I am in the emergency-response world. But at my core I will always be a firefighter and my ears will always perk up at the sound of that old, Second World War-era fire siren.

What helped quell the firefighter's adrenaline-fuelled autopilot function in me was my partner's and my decision to move to a bigger, more appropriate house for our family.

Because my kids were getting older and their living in the same room became more and more awkward for them, my partner and I (a few years before I went off work), looked for a place that had three bedrooms. We finally found a mini home we were quite taken with. So, after going through the lengthy and somewhat arduous process of buying, we packed up our things and set off on our new adventure.

This move would see me leaving my hometown after forty years. At one time, the very thought of leaving the town I loved would have seemed impossible. I'm certain that, if my life's path had gone in a direction that saw me more mentally fit, moving to a different town altogether would have been a definite "no." But since my life was infiltrated by mental illness, mostly made unbearable by being a firefighter in this same community, I was eager to leave. Maybe it was exactly what I needed, and starting fresh could be what would save me.

Would it? It was very helpful, and, I believe, it bought me a few good years working with a population I loved.

Today, the sounds of a fire engine's siren off in the distance or becoming ever louder as it heads my way, conjures up the symptoms of post-traumatic stress. What once was associated with "positivity," can now take me out of life for the day. I get that old familiar numb feeling and I can become easily startled and disassociated. What once fuelled huge desire to help, has been replaced by a feeling of internal helplessness, as I feel the shame and desire to want to continue with the duties given to me as a firefighter. Somewhere deep within, there is a disgraced young man who still believes I am strong enough to simply "Suck it up!" and go back. The wise old veteran knows better.

Finally, time put distance between me and the fire service. Within this gap, I began to realize that my plan to minimize my involvement with the dead by resigning from the department – and no matter how good and solid it was in my head – was far from being successful. I had learned I was much too late to salvage any semblance of the man I once knew.

It had gotten to be like a physical injury, one that could not be avoided. I was powerless to stop mental illness from consuming me, the hard-working, always-busy and helping person I had loved being. To top it all off – and to bring in a wartime analogy – I felt like a spent shell casing on the beaches of Normandy, all but abandoned and forgotten by those I had fought fire beside.

It Was Like Trying to Stop a Train, Five Feet From a Car on the Tracks

Only a year or two after my resignation from the fire department, I knew that I was on a slippery slope. Because I had neglected my mental health for so long, there was simply no turning back. At this point I was on an inevitable crash course with PTSD.

I came to this reality when I discovered that being a firefighter no longer worked to ease my mental pain. And I had been so hopeful that my grand plan would have worked, that I would have had the strength to enjoy the career I loved, to retirement. But choosing to remain in that environment only compounded my misery. I quickly would be overwhelmed and barely functional, to the point where I was calling in sick all the time and retreating more and more from the outside world.

As if by chance or fate my work environment became what was like the perfect storm. The unit slowly morphed into a mild but bad-enough behavioural unit for me. As the process of conversion took place overtime, I became more and more anxious as I knew that working with behaviours like these had been devastating for my mental health in the past. This may sound repetitive, but that's what it was, a constant battering.

Before long, I was once again working with so many of the clients I had worked with in the past. This made the environment even louder, and with it came a high risk of violence. As a consequence, my anxiety was being triggered every minute of every day I was there. In the end, it became so bad that by times my concentration levels were such that I couldn't even remember what I was doing from one moment to the next. Often it was just doing circles and trying to retrace my steps. I was in a numbed survival-like state, always on autopilot.

Like that of countless other people, I fooled myself into thinking that by hanging in there I was doing what was best for my family: I was wrong. At this time there was also a lot of political upheaval in the workplace. Scheduling changes and leadership deficits caused constant chaos on the unit, both for the residents and for their care providers. All of this, combined by the decisions that were being made, was so mentally draining and exhausting that what little strength I had left to battle on my own inner turmoil, was not sufficient enough to keep doing it day in and day out. I was caught in a tsunami of mental anguish.

The scheduling changes put me in a precarious position, not only mentally, but also personally. Because I didn't see my kids every day, my new schedule meant that I would go a significant period of time without seeing them at all. Now that it became personal, to me, the branch I was hanging on to was beginning to break, weakening, cracking, in such a way that it could have totally snapped at any moment. It was the only time that I can recall breaking down and crying in the workplace. I said to myself, "I have worked so hard to build a new life for my kids and me, and now my workplace is just going to take that all away?"

Luckily, I would be offered the opportunity to work one-on-one with a resident who was a danger to others. The upside of this? It allowed me to remain on the schedule I had worked with for years, and allowed me to see my kids with the consistency they needed and deserved, and that I needed and deserved.

In the beginning of this new venture as a one-to-one staff, I kept trying to convince myself that this was good for me, good for us. Fortunately, I wouldn't have to face the everyday upheavals that came with care for over twenty-four other people. I thought this would mean lower stimulus. As it would turn out, this new work assignment didn't inoculate me from the inside mess that was growing increasingly more dire as the days moved forward. The resident was extremely loud and was aggressive nearly every day. It pounded through my skull, and my body was always ready to charge and fight back.

Even so, I felt that I could endure it for a while, and I think that all things considered, I would have been able to keep going with no major problems or lasting damage.

However, a year into this assignment, my mental health and any reserves it contained would be tested like never before. In the fall of 2017, I would, yet again, come face to face with death's blank stare. It would seem that retiring from the fire service to avoid the most dreadful and tragic moments life has to offer, was in vain. That Thanksgiving I would desperately try and save the life of a man whose life came to a sad and sudden end, and with it, something in me died, like a silent falling snow. The accumulation of death after death crushed me under its weight.

CHAPTER FIFTEEN

A Not So Happy Thanksgiving

"Thanksgiving of 2017. The happy, simplistic life that I had worked so hard to build, came crashing down and I was powerless to stop it."

There's a social misnomer floating out there in the hearts and minds of all of us that says "humans are in charge of their own destinies." All my life I wanted this to be true. I wanted this to be the way things go. But I would come to learn that this social norm, which I'm sure may be true for some, is mere fiction to people like myself.

It seemed that the fate that is mental illness would have its way with me for what felt like the majority of my life. I often feel as if it had fooled me at times, while at others it had given me just enough leash to make it feel like I was free from its clutches. When I ran, for example, I was free. When I could feel the cool spring air on my face as I jogged, it seemed as though I left the anxieties' lies at the starting line. I was wrong. Other than when I was exercising, it was always in control, but like a demented soul, it ruled me, at points, in silence. With some of us, this mental-illness monster is built in.

When I was running and one with nature, I was able to manage the deeper, more painful side of myself for most of my adult life. With that said, when mental illness did come ashore, especially the PTSD, it was like a Category 5 hurricane, significantly changing my life's course. Really, my entire wellness journey's direction was changed with each debilitating episode, like the first time my anxiety disorder forced me out the door of my workplace. "You can knock me down but you'll never take me out."

Over The Edge I Go

In October of 2017, my family and I were invited to my aunt's home for Thanksgiving dinner. My partner at the time, my children and I, along with many others from my family – aunts, cousins and my mother and father – were all there. I remember it like it was yesterday. It was a perfect October afternoon. In the air was a comfy warm feeling that only a sunny fall day can bring. I was feeling both safe and excited to be in the company of my family.

What intensified the excitement was that I would finally get to spend time with my extended family. For most of my life, we had spent very little time together, so a part of me, undoubtedly my inner child, wanted to re-experience that safe, no-worries feeling I had when I was a kid, when we all gathered for special occasions just like this.

Feeling nostalgic about sitting down to dinner with people whom I hadn't gathered with in years, I really wanted to establish a connection that would be long-lasting. I was also hopeful "that a stronger family bond will help with this mental health journey," as I'd say to myself. Connection with people you love can make or break a person fighting a mental disorder.

At the same time in the fall of 2017, all sense of mental strength was being eroded by this constant barrage of critical incidents. For the best part of three years, we had lost so many of our clients to one cause of death or another, that it compounded a mid-level numbness I couldn't extinguish. Death is an inevitability when working in long-term care, but the already-tender mental injury in my head was broken open because of the past tragedies in the fire service. The heart attacks, the casualties due to fire and the countless scenes of crumbled metal and loss of life at accident scenes, had taken an enormous toll on me.

"I don't think I can handle any more trauma" often echoed in my head and did so, well before I took my last walk through the firehouse. Now this? All this pain floating around in my head was, and still is, like read-only files on a computer, those files in the brain that can't be erased.

The Moment The World Stood Still

While the smokers were outside doing their thing, I heard the muffled sound of a car door slam as the remaining members of my family were arriving for dinner. Shortly after their arrival, my dad came bursting into my aunt's poorly-lit living room. His eyes were wide and frantic, and the words tumbled out: "There's an old man dead on the front porch!"

I jumped to my feet. I didn't think anything at all, I simply reacted. With that old familiar feeling of adrenaline rushing through my veins, I shot right into firefighter autopilot, that second-nature reaction that sends all emergency workers into emergency helper mode. Our superpower.

Family members were crowded in the driveway and standing adjacent to the front porch, each of them bewildered and hands flapping helplessly, by what was taking place. I could also see the desperate looks that said, "What the hell do I do?"

When I turned to my left, my life changed forever in only seconds. Before me was indeed a male, bald, lying motionless on the approximately four-foot rail. He was just lying there, with the appearance of jaundice. His colour told me that what was playing out in front of us was bad, really bad. It was also at this moment that I stopped in my tracks as though someone had hit me in the chest with a sledgehammer. In those terrible moments, all time stood still. Even though my family was all around, I did not hear a sound, they simply de-materialized into the background. Afterwards I recall thinking, so this must be what it's like to go instantly deaf.

Trapped in a world of numbness and disassociation, I believe with all my heart that this was the day both the firefighter and healthcare worker in me finally died. I feel strongly that this was what awoke my PTSD because ever since, I've spent the majority of my time at home, attempting to avoid any potential catastrophe that can occur in the world. "John, what are you doing? This is not living!"

Not long after I froze, I heard my aunt's voice off in the distance say, "John, help him." It was then I realized that I was the only person there with the experience and training to do something. With my voice flat and shaky, and with my legs feeling heavy as lead, I think I told someone to call 911.

As I made my way to the steps, there were only two things I can remember. It felt like I was wading through molasses as I made my way up the stairs, each step thick and heavy with absolute dread. And as I made my way closer to this man, I could see that he was sitting in one of those white, flexible lawn chairs slumped over and head still resting on the railing. I recall telling myself, "You can do this! After all, you have dealt with death dozens and dozens of times, so man up!"

What I found so different from the normal accumulative numbness and brain fog that I experienced over the course of my firefighting career, was this in- and out-of-reality sensation. It was like that of a movie trailer that for a second fades to black and has its scene come back on-screen, but in a slightly-advanced shot, like it moved forward just a bit. The entire incident was met, for me, with this never before-felt semi-shutdown effect.

My brain's semi-shutdown only intensified as I stood over this man, who had only moments earlier been alive. I went from "You can do this" to "You can't do this, and you knew that for a long time."

By the time I reached the man, my cousin had joined me, silent. The only time he spoke was to ask me if I needed a hand. At the same time, the 911 operator had advised me to start CPR. "Let's lay him down, gently," I said.

With me at the man's head and my cousin taking the feet, we lay him down as carefully and respectfully as possible. It wasn't until he was lying at my feet that I saw that in fact, this wasn't an old man at all, but rather a person who looked to be in the prime of his life. Late twenties, early thirties. In that moment, it was like some unseen entity reached down and yanked my heart and soul right out of my body.

I stood there frozen. I didn't realize it that day, but later I would learn that the helper as I knew him, the one my entire identity was built around, also expired that day, right next to this unfortunate person.

I am certain to this day that my mentally-lifeless self would have stayed there, almost catatonic forever, if it weren't for my mother. Somehow, she must have sensed that I was so deep into an alternate state that she felt compelled to come closer to me than anyone else did. Although I was essentially written off, I still noticed her instantly. She was standing at the bottom of the steps looking up at me. I remember this because she's all I could see. I looked at her and said, "He's dead." I would later interpret this statement to mean that there was no saving him.

Once she got a good look at me, she obviously knew by my pale face and blank stare that I was done, and not just for that moment. Maybe she even saw that this sort of instant damage would take years to recover from.

I remember her saying, "Son, come down from there. It's all right." She later told me that she knew something in me had changed that evening, something long lasting and damning. As always, Momma was right.

So Surreal

On a cognitive level, I know that there was so much more that took place in those terrible moments, but just can't remember them. As my mind tried to make sense of what lay before it, it was, at the same time, trying to save me. From what? From myself and the mass accumulation of tragic events I had been involved with over the course of my adult life.

What made this very sudden and devastating death so surreal for me was a combination of its timing and my own disintegrating mental health, specifically surrounding trauma.

I remember, once I made my way off the steps, going inside and just hugging my kids and trying to explain to my partner what had taken place. My tone was sharp, and I grew impatient, as if everything must take place asap.

"What went on out there?" came the avid voice.

"A young man died on the porch," I said sharply.

"Uh...okay, he died?"

With a short pause and tears building in my eyes, I said "Yes!" That was all I could force past the lump in my throat.

I think I was feeling trapped as I struggled to make sense of what had taken place only a few feet from where we were all sitting down to a beautifully-prepared dinner. Odd that I never thought about leaving. I suppose my cognitive reasoning had given way to some sort of survival mechanism. Here we all were, sitting down at the table, each with a heaping plate of turkey, potatoes, carrots and turnip. Surreal, jumping back into life as though nothing had happened. All the while, I was feeling trapped and angry, partly because this man passed away on "today of all days." Why?

Another part of me was so agitated with myself because I, the firefighter, was not able to help save this life and on this day we are supposed to be giving thanks for all that is good in life. Mostly, though, I was a hybrid of heartbroken and very-pissed at the fact that I kept saying to myself, "You weren't supposed to see anyone die like this again. You are a civilian now, for God's sake!" I guess PTSD's power to debilitate me, and my sensitive disposition, were destined to change my life forever.

The one thing I am grateful for? That my kids were oblivious to the events that took place that horrific night. I was hell-bent on ensuring that they remained that way. "They're just kids and they are both sensitive like me. This would cause real damage."

To this day, the thing I find the most surreal about this young man's passing is how we picked up and carried on with "business as usual." Thinking of it still numbs me to my core.

Because the cause of death was undetermined at the time, this man lay on the step for the entire evening under police guard while we, as a family, all sat down to eat. We chatted, we laughed, albeit in a much more subdued way. Despite this heavy feeling that dominated the holiday, we tried our best to make a go of it. "Pass the potatoes, John" I recall one of my aunts saying.

About halfway through the meal, there was a knock on the door. It was an RCMP officer checking in on us. The second he came in the door I heard him say, "Ummm, it sure smells wonderful in here."

I don't know why, but as soon as he emerged, I gravitated towards him. I recall saying, "Would you like a piece of pie?"

He said, "I'd love a piece. Haven't eaten since lunch."

I know that deep inside, everyone there that day was in shock and mourning. I think giving thanks was the only thing we could do. To the end, I will remain stuck on the thought that, "While we carried on, this man's own family would have their lives torn to shreds." And then, "The ache I felt and still feel for you is immeasurable. I hope you will be able to find some semblance of peace."

And I can't help but feel that this tragedy happening on a holiday intensified my trauma. After all, traumatic events and special occasions aren't supposed to mesh together. They don't mix well. It's a moment and time in my life that I will never forget. Part of me remains broken for a man that I was too ill to save.

CHAPTER SIXTEEN

Losing My Grip

"Oh my God, I think I have PTSD. Didn't matter I had a family to support."

As the fall slowly turned into winter, with its gradually-dropping temperatures and moderate snowfall, I found myself living more outside my body than in it. The best way I can describe this "out-of-body experience" is a feeling of looking at yourself, but being aware that, somehow, you are still in your body. It's heavy and light all at the same time. Sometimes I feel as if my surroundings are closing in on me like some medieval booby trap. Other times, the world feels bigger than it should.

Shortly after that Thanksgiving, I remember telling myself that "this will pass within a week." I was wrong. By the time the lights and hustle and bustle of the Christmas period rolled around, I would come to my own conclusion that I had been stricken with the mental-health condition of post-traumatic stress disorder.

Despite my suspicions, I, like the tough guy I thought I was, continued to ignore the signs and symptoms and to plow through my day like a footballer on the field. I thought to myself that because I had been "inflicted upon" by mental illness in the past, I would know exactly when I had enough. While this is partially true, it turns out that in the long run, PTSD would make the choice for me. Over the coming year, I would learn that this is no easy illness. In fact, I came to say, "Post-traumatic stress disorder is an entirely different beast."

Somehow, despite feeling I was being squished in a vice, with my mental pain slowly becoming heavier, I came to a crossroads that winter. As a matter of trying to figure out where I was on the scale of mental-illness severity, I was reaching out to co-workers and friends in an attempt to assess the damage. While my co-workers and friends had absolutely no idea how to address the conversations, I was having with them, their kindness did allow me to get through almost an entire year after the event.

While I was oblivious at the time, I had mistaken symptoms of post-traumatic stress disorder for absent-mindedness. So did my coworkers. It wasn't until after I buckled under the weight of mental illness, that I realized I was being re-traumatized, over and over, by the violence and the near-constant noise of my workday. This shutdown would put me into fight, flight or freeze mode and screw up my cognitive ability to perform even the most mundane of tasks. The best way to describe this cognitive impairment is to imagine what you feel like when hit on the head. The force most certainly throws you and leaves you stunned. Noise and aggression made me feel a lot like that, only I felt I was continuously being pounded by a form of blunt-force trauma from the inside out.

I wish I had known at the time that not too far ahead lay yet more broken track. It was just lying there, waiting for us to meet up and for it to keep tossing me into some mental hellish state. My preoccupation and numbness of brain fog would slap blinders over my eyes, not allowing me to see the dangers ahead. On top of this, I still had to pay bills and feed my children.

I would come to learn that with mental pain this intense, there's little to no chance of getting beyond it unscathed. And by the following September, my abilities to keep moving forward would fail me. As a result, my entire life as I knew it would finally plow over these damaged tracks at full speed and into a ravine too deep to climb out of.

It Took Only a Moment

At the beginning of September of 2018, my life would change forever. I can recall the exact moment when the brittle wall I had built around me came tumbling down and crumbling to dust.

I was in the middle of shop-steward training for the union I was in. It was at this juncture where I was looking for opportunities to remove myself from the work environment, more often through training. That way I thought I could find more balance by still being employed, yet not being on the unit nearly as often. I would not make it three weeks after the course, and before I knew it, would be making my way home from work for the very last time.

The moment my perceived strength and PTSD collided, was when someone at the shop-steward training was explaining how they were looking for a client who had run away from our care facility He explained, "He ran away, and of course, nowadays you can't bring them back to the Centre – you can only keep an eye on them once you do find them." During their search, they explained, they had discovered a deceased individual lying in the woods. "He was just lying there...finding him was so unexpected."

As soon as I heard they had found a body, I was immediately transported back to that past Thanksgiving – when I had disengaged from all reality on the front porch of my aunt's apartment building, standing over a young man who passed way too soon.

Only aware that I was now still physically sitting there, with the shop steward, I could feel my inner self jump up and run out the door.

From that moment forward, everything around me once again de-materialized into the background. When this happens, it's like the feeling of tunnel vision or one of those dreams where you can't move your eyes up or down, cheated out of a full three-hundred and sixty degree view of what you're dreaming about.

The man next to me must have seen my non-present stare because he immediately, gently, put his hand on my shoulder and said, "If you need to go outside, that's okay." His gentle concern thrust me back into the moment. It had the same kind of effect as waking from sleep. Thanks to his keen eye and his authentic concern, I was able to complete the rest of the day.

You probably know the exact moment when mentally you can take no more, in whatever the situation. I now knew in the back of my mind that I had to plan my immediate exit from that unforgiving environment. In that defining moment, I knew that I was traumatized and was nearly at the crescendo of a mental-health emergency. I knew the moment had come when I couldn't fight any more.

From that day forward, I would set a plan in motion that would allow me to exit my workplace in such a way that once I was better, I could return. I would accomplish this goal through professional negotiations between myself, my union reps and my managers.

After consulting with the union, it became clear to me that I needed to enlist the help of a mental-health professional, and was told "In order for you to go off on sick leave, you need to be officially diagnosed with something."

"But I already had a diagnosed anxiety disorder," I said.

"Yes," my reps replied. "But that was years ago. It would hold more weight if you went back to mental health. If you do have PTSD, you will have a better case."

So, in only a matter of weeks after I met with the union, I once again found myself face-to-face with my doctor, the general practitioner. She put in a referral to mental health and addiction services and before I knew it, I was sitting across from a newly-graduated psychiatrist. Crisply, professionally dressed, this average-sized woman with a gentle voice quickly diagnosed me with major depressive disorder. Despite my true intentions of seeing her, which was to determine whether I had post-traumatic stress disorder or not, she was unable to diagnose me with that then. Nonetheless, I had a diagnosis. "Your affect and low mood for long periods of time, says to me that you have MDD."

A diagnosis was so important, because to make it possible for me to go off work and still retain my position, I would have to be diagnosed with a mental-health disorder. But...receiving a diagnosis of major depressive disorder was a complete and utter surprise to me. In fact, it wasn't even on my radar. Depression? "Depression?" I said disbelievingly to myself.

As I delved into the research on major depressive disorder, I began to see myself within the literature, and not only at that present moment. It explained a lot throughout my entire life. I began to figure out that depression had indeed been my travel companion since I was a boy, or at least as far back as I could remember.

The Light-Bulb Moment

As this revelation became clear, I began to see there was a deep-seated sadness extending way back to when I was a schoolboy. Acting out and being aggressive towards objects could now, without question, be put down to depression. If I had known this back then, and if the adults in my life had seen past the observable behaviours, perhaps my life would have taken a turn for the better. Nonetheless, here I was, learning at the age of forty-two, that this dark menace that followed me for all of my life was a mental-health condition – a depressive disorder.

With this light-bulb moment and recalling the feelings of lonely and inexplicable sadness as a youngster and beyond, it explained why my life always ran in the opposite direction in which I would have loved it to go. My home life was a perfect example of things not going the way I had dreamed of. My parents' dedicating their lives to feeding and clothing my sister was a good example.

And while their need to constantly work to meet our physical needs was an understandable priority, it nonetheless cultivated the sad and lonely way I felt within and would do so just from their long absence from home. As a result, this elusive mental hardship would fester just under the surface, remaining undefined and going undiagnosed for decades. My folks were doing their best and, in the end, did get me help. However, despite their efforts, this growing predisposition to mental illness likely was unstoppable.

My folks didn't see it, the teachers didn't see it and I had no skills to recognize it in myself. To these adults, all I had were "anger issues." Unruly children should be disciplined, was the popular notion in those days. Too bad they failed to recognize that punitive action was a bit like putting water to a plant. It not only kept the turmoil within me alive and well, it helped to grow it stronger and so much more resilient.

Because things played out the way they did, I wound up spending what felt to me like most of my time alone. Through no fault of anyone really, I did normalize feeling down to such an extent I thought that the way I was feeling, was the way I was supposed to feel. I mean, doesn't everyone feel this way?

My Graceful Exit

Convinced more than ever that I needed to take care of myself, I finally called a meeting with my management and union. When the day of the meeting came, we all sat at a boardroom table. Here I was with my union reps, sitting to my left and right, looking across the table at the five managers seated practically in a row, all with perplexed looks on their faces and just sitting there in silence.

Once we all were ready, we laid it all out for them. My rep on the right, a fellow around my age, with short salt-and-pepper, hair, articulated my reasons for meeting with them the best. He explained that I was diagnosed with depression and what had taken place the previous Thanksgiving. He went on to tell his colleagues that not only was I suffering from major depression, I was actively pursuing a diagnosis of PTSD. By the time I was sitting in this boardroom with everyone who controlled my fate all gathered around, I began to shake, convincing myself that they were going to be difficult. It felt like a huge "something" I was too frail to deal with at that time..

What made this so unnerving for me was knowing that the director of nursing, the one who'd been so compassionate, and understanding, had retired a few years back. So, not only did I not know what to expect from these people, it seemed that the current leadership was less inclined to extend those same levels of compassion and support. I was right to feel the way I did.

I recall the newly hired HR person saying, "Um, excuse me, I fail to see why we are all here..?"

That's when the rep said, "We are here today because John has recently been diagnosed with depression and he says it's so bad that he needs to take time off to get help and get better."

The looks on their faces went from, "Why are we here?" to "And we are all here because...?" I'm guessing they felt it wasn't necessary for all of them to be there for that.

The new director said, "I'm sorry to hear that, John. You need to apply for Long Term and go from there."

While they were far from cold, the meeting felt "all business" to me and made me uncomfortable. This time round, I did not receive the support I had gotten years before. The most solid piece of advice they gave me, and one they kept repeating, was to go on long-term disability. Even the staff health nurse echoed their suggestion. "John, I really think if you are finding coming to work really difficult, that's what LTD is for."

With that, they wished me good luck and called the meeting to an end. My last day at work, the place I had sacrificed and given my entire adult life to, ended in less than an hour on September 18th, 2018.

My exit, while appearing abrupt and too numbing to be disappointing in that moment, was nonetheless done the right way. After the management had left the board room, I recall saying to my union reps, "You guys really went all out for me. Thank you so much. I will never forget it."

The gentlemen to my left said, "That's what we are here for. You need to look out for yourself and by coming to us, you now know that your job is safe."

The other man who sat off to my right, extended his hand and said, "You're welcome, sir. If there's anything else we can do to help, you know where we are."

We as a team, the union and I, were able to ensure they held my position. With so much going on in respect to my mental health, this was a huge burden lifted off my shoulders. I will always remember the hard work those two fellas put in on my behalf. Before I left, I thanked them once again and with a heavy heart headed for the door. While taking this step to secure my employment was a smart move, I felt an underlying sense of relief cover my constant feeling of dread with a thin layer of freedom. Because my workplace played such a role in the decline of my health, after this sit-down with my bosses, I felt like a caged lion that had finally been set free on the sub-Saharan land mass of Africa. It was in this moment that I felt as if I was once again on the road to mental wellness. "Now I can seek out answers without worrying about coming to work," I said to myself.

Walking away from my profession wasn't new for me but this time around. it was met with intense uncertainty. Even though some of my fears were put at ease, I was nonetheless plagued with the thought of "What if I can't get myself well enough to return? What if I have PTSD and it's the end of my life as I know it?" The remarkable story-telling power of anxiety was surging through every fibre of my being by the time I had walked, yet again, out those industrial, glass-and aluminum-framed doors and out to my car.

Even though I was walking into the unknown, I can't even begin to describe the feeling of relief that came over me. I found this odd because I was also scared as hell. "Now what are you going to do, John? Do what you gotta do, as always."

What I didn't realize at the time was just how ill I had become. So, by the time I got to my car on that warm September day, I thought of not having to go back into that loud and often-violent work-space. Coming to this reality was nothing short of liberating and with it, a calm and peaceful feeling came over me in waves. Never forget that feeling! "Sad, really, you schmuck," I said to myself, "That you had to get to a point where you could take no more before you walked away and did what was best for you, and ultimately your family."

CHAPTER SEVENTEEN

Into the Abyss

"The most difficult moments for me during my journey? The moments when I had absolutely no idea where to turn, the moments when I felt I had no control in the course of my own destiny."

Arriving home, I looked up from the wheel and at our sixty-six-foot mini home with its faded grey vinyl siding and burgundy shutters. I remember that as I stared at it, I said to myself, "I could hide out in you forever." Since that tragic Thanksgiving, my fear had escalated to such a degree that I was beginning to be "okay" with remaining behind closed doors and tucked away from everything that breathed.

I had reached a point where the many tragic events I had witnessed were so toxic, they completely engulfed my mind. I was so eaten with worry that I might have to help save someone, that I was absolutely terrified at the prospect of any emergency situation that "might" arise. It was then, as I sat numbly in my driveway, that I decided my sanctuary lay just beyond the white door at the front of the home. "I'd be okay with staying home forever." I said to myself as I got out of the car and made my way to the house.

For the next few weeks following my departure from work, I felt like I had walked into a sea of nothingness. All I wanted was to lie in bed and hope things would sort themselves out. I hoped that my long bouts of sleep would cause my trauma to somehow melt away, and I would rise from the dark and be cured.

With the nature of mental illness working against me as mental illness so often does, this hopeful notion ended up being a dose of wishful thinking. I do recall near the end of my sabbatical, giving myself a verbal kick in the ass, telling myself that a cure for my ailments wouldn't happen on its own. "John, with your counselling background and your battle with mental illness, you know that doing nothing will not make you better. You have battled your way back from the darkness before, so get moving! You can do this again."

With that, my stubbornness would come crashing into my head like a drill sergeant, screaming and hollering the mantra that had always, without fail, dug me out of the darkest times in my life. This was a very clear message, a message of "What do you have to do to get better?"

Well, for once, my goal was pretty clear. I had to seek whatever help was available to me to see me through my most taxing battle to date. With that knowledge, I applied for WCB, Workers' Compensation Board, benefits. If I could get the diagnosis, I was blaming for my mental health decline, that of PTSD, then I would qualify for this compensation. And because I was a firefighter with a diagnosis, I automatically would be granted the payments.

Although it may have taken me several months to admit that my trauma was whittling away at my wellness, I finally caved and conceded. Doing so gave me the very strength I needed to take the route of workers' compensation.

This was a place I had railed so hard against to avoid. After all, I was capable, strong, and made of titanium, right? PTSD would prove to be a more than formidable foe, so strong in fact, that it would take the WCB route or die. Death is something I rail even harder against.

While I was diligently attempting to get WCB, I remembered my union rep, the one who sat to my right in the meeting with management and did such a good job speaking on my behalf. He had told me I should apply for both workers' compensation and long-term disability.

I did so out of fear. Now that I knew for certain that I wasn't going back to work in the foreseeable future, my reality then became that of this: "I need help to keep the roof over my family's heads." Not knowing whether one will have an income or not was, of course, fuel for the ole anxiety disorder. Oh, the horror stories it wrote in my head while my life was in limbo.

In my world, anxiety has always been a funny thing, I would be so anxious over moments like these, yet, at the same time, I was driven to compulsion to do what I had to do to solve it. Even now, I think my chief motivator is to push past how anxiety makes me feel, as quickly and as painlessly as possible. Anxiety is typically driven by avoidance and while there was certainly lots of that going on, I just couldn't and still can't deal with that constant dread and preconceived rejection and/or those thoughts of failure.

I guess it's the "tearing off the band-aid" phenomenon for me. Ripping that sucker off like a reckless fool hurt like anything, but only for a few seconds. In contrast, a slow peeling leaves a longer, more drawn-out painful experience. This is how I've learned to combat GAD, generalized anxiety disorder, and well, any other form of mental pain. Doing what has to be done is not only quicker, but it's also more bearable than simply trying to cope using denial and avoidance.

I guess my approach to this particular disorder paid dividends. Because the red tape and all the procedures that accompany filing for compensation was daunting, I wanted to get through that pain as quickly as possible. So I was prompt at getting it done. And all the appointments that were also required were equally heavy. I felt like the equivalent to a worn-out punching bag, being beaten on from two sides.

I gave it my all on days I was well enough to, and rested on the days I was symptomatic. This turned out to be the right move for me and because it provided me the energy to go the distance, I am able to credit this method to my success. If there's one thing I've learned through this lifelong ordeal it's that, like a physical disability, mental disabilities also need a customized approach to achieve what needs to be done. That includes, but is not limited to, seeking out a new purpose for a new way of life. There were days where I was so overcome because of nightmares the night before that I found myself saying, "It's okay that you have to stay in bed today. Just remember, one or two days of rest are good. After that, back to the battle."

I'm happy that I learned to do what I could on the days I was able and did not try to push forward on a relentless pursuit to get the help I needed. I know I would never have been able to keep pace. If not up for what I had planned to tackle the next day – and as long as it wasn't a mandatory appointment for an assessment – I would give myself permission to say "the hell with it." I'm grateful I learned that lesson.

The Anticipated Bumps in the Road

Because I had looked for counsel from some outside advocacy groups – i.e., one that fights on behalf of those trying to get WCB – I anticipated some bumps in the road and thanks to them, I was ready for it, or at least prepared for hiccups.

I had good support every step of the way in having to go off work and seeking out help with compensation. There also was the "plus" of being mentally ill in my past. Does that sound crazy? Yes, it was a benefit. Why? Because I had learned that the mental-health system is severely underfunded and hard to get into. It leaves two choices. One, that I give up, which meant I would be giving up on myself, my family, and with it, any shot I'd have had at recovery and returning to work. Two, that I advocate for myself and get the help I need.

I learned how to fight for myself the first time I went off work with my anxiety disorder. Finding my voice early on in my wellness journey would prove to be a great tool – a rope, a pick-axe, a parachute – in the face of this mountainous climb I had before me this time around.

Knowing that everything mental health-related comes with challenges, it came as no surprise that WCB wanted me to see one of their own psychologists to determine whether I had PTSD or not. Equally not surprising was their appointed therapist determining that I was not suffering from post-traumatic stress disorder. Wrong! I'm no mental-health clinician, but coming from a counselling background, I do know that no psychologist I know of could make a fair and accurate assessment in a thirty-minute intake session.

Once we got down to the crux of the reason I was sitting in her cramped and dim office, our time was probably eroded down to fifteen minutes. Some small talk, a little about my reasons for suspecting PTSD…and then she looked at me and said, "I don't think you have PTSD. I will have a report sent to your case worker by Monday."

As I went out and into my car, I knew what I had to do. First, I refused to let that therapy session – like speed dating – torpedo my future. I wouldn't hang my head and accept her assessment. My life was at stake.

The therapist told me her report would be done and handed into WCB the following Monday, early December, but it didn't arrive and get in the hands of my case manager until early January. The day it arrived? I felt my body go rigid with shock. This lengthy report was consistently inaccurate. My traumatic incidents I had explained to her from over my fire-service days, specifically, the ones that still haunt me, were all blended together as one incident. The genders were wrong, and personal details were either missing or just unbelievably wrong. "What the hell! Did she get me mixed up with someone else?"

"You don't care," I thought, feeling the pain of it like being sucker-punched. My case had gotten pushed to the bottom of the pile and because of it, her assessment was written in haste. To date, this is the most irresponsible, most uncaring thing I have had to endure by a mental-health professional, by someone who calls themselves a professional. Helpless to fight against it, I said to myself, "This kind of thing could damage someone, really kill them."

Feeling the anger pumping in my veins, and driven by my background as a counsellor, I called my WCB case manager, a soft-spoken man, whom I have never laid eyes on. When he answered the phone, he was met with my loud but professionally-delivered rant: "Have you received the psychologist's assessment yet?

He evidently had received the report that same day because he said to me – or at least this is all I remember – that "Your claim is being denied, John, based on the psychologist's assessment."

I just plunged into a tirade – about all the errors in the assessments. "Oh man! How can you deny my claim based on what was a fifteen-minute session and a report that was so inaccurate that I thought it was someone else?" Can't recall all I said – it's somewhere there in an awful black hole – but I finished off by saying, "I will win on appeal."

His response was a swift "I will talk to my manager."

Finally, a Beacon of Light

I will always be grateful that I applied for both workers' compensation and long-term disability. I'm also grateful for the psychologist's delay with her report, because in January of 2019, I started to get help from the long-term program as well.

No surprise to me that long-term disability wanted me to see their own psychologist. This would be a pivotal moment in my recovery. I finally had discovered a therapist willing to invest the time and energy to find out through clinical assessments whether I was post-traumatic or not. So, during my rant with my caseworker, I brought this up to him.

A few days later, the WCB case worker got back to me and told me that because I was going to see another psychologist, whatever that therapist concluded, they would accept. Not only would they accept her written assessment, but they would also pay any fees incurred to have a copy of that assessment.

I often reflect on this moment in time, a blip on the radar in terms of my life span, but still a huge turning point. Despite being kicked and punched by mental illness to the degree it had me on the ropes, I still recognized that I had to be my own advocate. Pushing myself so that I would survive literally saved my life. Had I failed to understand that I am it, that I must put what energy I did have into getting better, I would literally have lain down and died. For me, it would have like been standing in front of a monstrous wave. If you stand there long enough, you will eventually come to terms with the fact that you are out of time and let the wave take you. So, even if moving forward offered little hope, I still chose to keep moving.

There's an Actual Assessment for That?

When the day came to sit in front of the psychologist provided to me by long-term disability, I sensed right away that we could establish a good rapport. Sometimes you just know.

My intuition proved to be correct. Much to my excitement and overwhelming relief, this mental-health provider refused to hastily make any snap clinical decisions. In fact, she decided that she would not render a decision based on observation, but rather, she chose to implement diagnostic tools. These were assessments based on scores and tailored toward specific disorders, one of which was for PTSD. With having felt sick, cheated and disbelieved for so long, I suddenly said to myself, "My dream. My dream psychologist." Yes! I had been through so much, and this, this woman was the psychologist I'd been looking for all my life.

There were multiple sessions and three assessments, one for depression, one for generalized anxiety disorder, and a third to determine whether I had post-traumatic stress disorder or not. We spent many hours, exhausting ones, going through these clinical tools for answers.

Can you believe I was elated that we were finally getting to the root of the problems I was experiencing? And out of all the clinicians, psychologists, psychiatrists and counsellors I had seen, this was the first professional person to ever put in a significant amount of work to find more definitive answers. Her approach to my mental health was exactly what I was looking for – if I had even known how to describe it – since I fell ill with my anxiety disorder all those years ago. "It was worth the long battle," I often say to myself when I think about this juncture in my life's story.

I can recall sitting in her well-lit office, with us across from one another in in chairs that, to me, were a pleasure to sit in. No doubt those walls had been painted that baby-blue to create a more calming and relaxing environment. If so, they worked, and I was able to better cope with the process. Facing a barrage of questions, session after session, had wrung me out, so much so that I was stricken with disassociation and once again felt I had tunnel vision, and that everything in my peripheral vision did not exist. The only thing I could hear was the sound of her voice.

Steady, calm, quiet. "And so, John, now we can look at this as..."

On occasion, I would come back to the present and from there, we continued on with the work needed to start my healing.

Stressed because it took longer than I anticipated to get to the end results, I was feeling bad that I was taking so long to work through these three assessments. But the triggers came constantly, and at times I was so tired that I was falling asleep. No doubt she had anticipated this. Her patient and professional approach was like a calming tonic to this hungry man.

She had long curly black hair and rounded glasses, and I tried to focus. "John, I see that you are tired. Do you want me to read the questions out loud for you?" She must have seen the look of relief on my face because before I could say anything she held out her hand and said, "Here, hand me the questions."

About halfway through, I gave myself permission to officially recognize how mentally exhausting this process was, and to sleep for hours after each session. Because I slept away my trauma, I was able to tough it out.

Her approach was perfect for what I needed at that time. Other than regular visits to the psychiatrist, I was receiving zero intervention for months. This was brutal, like spending the majority of my days hiding in the perceived safety of my home. However, the long wait was bittersweet because it made me even more grateful for her help every time I landed in her office.

Her therapeutic approach, a combination of these diagnostic tools, talk therapy and skill building, righted the ship in a sense, filling me with hope and providing me with a more clearly-defined direction. Until I saw her, I felt lost in a sea of despair, slowly drowning as I weakened from trying to keep my head from going under. The undertow had just been too great – but not great enough.

The Verdict

After a month of exhausting but ground-breaking work, the assessments were completed, and the conclusions were made. The verdict? In her professional opinion, based on these therapeutic diagnostic tools, she determined that "Jonathan Arenburg does indeed have post-traumatic stress disorder." The testing also revealed and confirmed the psychiatrist's diagnosis that I was also battling major depressive disorder. Topping it all off, like extra swirls of icing on a cake, was the confirmation of generalized anxiety disorder.

At the time I was more relieved that the assessment process was over than I was about the fact I was diagnosed with what I had suspected all along, PTSD. I have never been more tired in my entire life.

With assessments in hand, I left her office in a state, wondering just exactly what I felt. Happy? No. Sad? No. Angry? Not at all. Where, then is the word? How does one feel after being diagnosed with mental illnesses? If I had to sum up how I was feeling at the time with one word, I would have to say "relieved." All I really wanted was to have the mechanisms in place to start my road to mental wellness. Finally, I felt as if I had turned the corner – leaving litter behind and in its rightful containers – and was at the beginning of a healing journey.

It couldn't have been more than a week after the diagnosis when I heard back from Workers' Compensation. Because I finally had my diagnosis and had PTSD, my caseworker informed me "You have been approved for benefits, John." At around the same time, I also got approved for long-term disability as well. But because WCB had approved me first, Long

Term simply provided a top-up to be on par with my working wages.

After all that, I needed a long period to recuperate from this drawn-out battle. Finally, the bureaucracy was over, and like yanking off a rock that was chained to my ankle and holding me underwater, this granting of benefits finally allowed me to break free from the weight of uncertainty.

To my disappointment, the verdict came with a price. Now that I was officially on WCB, I had to see a psychologist that *they* provided. Because they were paying the majority of my benefits, I had to stop seeing the LTD therapist. More erosion, eating away at my chest, my brain – that's what it felt like. Torn apart again. Now I couldn't continue my road to recovery with a psychologist with whom I had built a fantastic rapport. We had been making inroads and I was feeling *good* about the therapeutic direction we were heading in.

Discouraged and angry, I was starting to feel that this whole process was nothing more than going from the basement to the first floor and back to the basement again. I thought, "Damn it, just as I am finally making progress." From progress to upheaval, and all it brought with it, once again.

Not only was I having to face these obstacles to care, I felt as if I was acting like a broken record, repeating the same thing over and over; sitting across from one mental health professional or another, constantly reliving and then repetitively being triggered by re-telling the tragic and gruesome details of my adult experience. Living through September to the beginning of March was pure hell. Some things have fallen into the black void of forgetfulness, but I remembered enough.

I felt as if I had reached the cliff-side of despair, the end. I could feel the exhaustion in every bone, every pore. From the nightmares and numbness to the bureaucratic processes I had to suffer, I was on my knees and ready to tap out. "That's it," I said. "Can't take any more. This is finally it."

While I seemed to be teetering on the edge, a whole inventory of why I chose to fight on, just seemed to plop into my head. It was my kids, my mother, father and sister, all those wonderful friends who had gotten me through the toughest aspects of my life, and saved me time and time again.. In fact, it was quite a crowd – and it seemed they all wished me well, in this movie scene that seemed to play in my head.

And from that, from somewhere, came the juice I needed to grab, drink, and step away from the edge. Since then, I have vowed that I would fight on with everything I had. Everyone I love became the shot in the arm I needed to keep going.

Feeling charged with a sense of purpose, I decided to embrace the long-awaited reprieve that came with the end of the bureaucratic endeavour. Finally, I had the finances I needed to keep the bill collectors at bay. Beyond that, and perhaps even more important, were the official diagnoses.

Armed with answers and a direction to head in, I began to move away from feeling hopeless and began to think of my transition to a new psychologist as a brand-new start. "One thing I have learned in my years on this earth," I said to myself, "is that perspective is everything." Taking the "blank slate" approach stifled my symptoms while at the same time, it gave me the strength to walk through the doors of my new therapist's office.

CHAPTER EIGHTEEN

Finally, a Glimmer of Normality

"Never giving up on yourself will get you the help you need."

With a fresh perspective and feeling everything had been put in place, I felt my hands close around the wheel of my own destiny. I felt terror at the thought of opening up once again to yet another stranger, but even with that, knew there would be few if any barriers to moving in a certain direction. "That," I said, "is the triumphant comeback to the world I was forced to abandon. A hell of a direction, the best one."

This fear was less than the worried feeling circulating around in my head. The psychologist was, after all, a WCB psychologist. I felt that my worry was valid. That initial experience with the first WCB therapist was, I thought, an attempt to railroad my healing. I really felt they were doing their best to ensure I was denied benefits. That would have denied me the resources I so desperately needed. Later, I would come to find out that one symptom of PTSD was lack of trust, or more specifically, of meeting things with an unhealthy dose of suspicion.

So, I approached this therapist with cautious optimism. For starters, I had no choice but to walk through that door as there was no other avenue to pursue. The only exception was my psychiatrist. But her role was to find the right regimen of medications to help me cope, to provide me with psychotherapeutic intervention, not therapy. "Still," I said, "I remain grateful for your help. You were the only hope I had for months."

The First Session

On the day of the first session, my fight-or flight response completely took over my mind, throwing me back into fantasy-land. The main theme of this anxiety-fuelled story-line being tossed around in my head was that of WCB. I became near-convinced that the therapist would look for any reason to discard me and leave me a wounded heap on my own.

I felt my nerves stretched to the nth degree, by the time I got to the therapist's office. As usual, I arrived early. But having an anxiety disorder and being diligent proved to be even more challenging than I figured. My early arrival had shut me down. Here I'd put myself in an unknown environment, that had my entire future as well as mental health in its hands. In therapist talk, it's "trauma-induced silence." I thought while I waited.

I only knew I was stewing away in my own stress, and thinking and believing things that weren't true.

I walked into yet another waiting room. Open-concept style, eggshell walls, blue-cushioned chairs with wood frames. They were in two rows, one firm against the wall and the other about four feet apart, facing the others.

After filling out the required paperwork and handing it back to the clerk, I came back to reality long enough to take note of the face and fellow behind the chest-high desk. His voice was made for radio and he had a larger-than-life laugh to go with it.

Once again, taking my seat, I tried desperately to slow my mind. Of course, it was going too fast to catch up with. Feeling like a caged animal, I was just about to jump out of my chair and run out the door, when I heard a female voice call out from behind me: "John!" Then "Come in and have a seat."

Too late to make a swift exit. I immediately said, "It's go time!"

I turned to the voice, and saw a woman about five feet tall, with a friendly face and long sandy hair, standing in the doorway of what I assumed was her office. As I made my way past her I saw how unremarkable it was. It reminded me of the average everyday bedroom in many homes – square, with white walls and a large window across from the door. The only thing that made this small space un-bedroom-like was the two chairs, semi-facing one another against one wall, and a desk, with papers and office items, directly across from where the therapy takes place. The other thing that stuck out to me was her display of credentials on the wall.

Fighting with myself not to run like hell, I reluctantly took a seat as she did. Probably sensing I was a mess, she introduced herself. "And now, John, I'd like you to begin telling me a bit about the events in my life that have landed you in my office".

Feeling a bit like a compact disk stuck on "repeat," I once again explained the series of events that had plunged me into this state of being – low tolerance, hyper-vigilant, terrified of death. "I think my years in the fire service and the nonstop violence I attempted to mitigate every day in my work environment has destroyed me," I told her.

As many times as I ran down all the traumatic incidents that had come together like the perfect storm, and running me off the road of life, it never got easier, never. Repeating the same tragic memories over and over always evoked the same numb and mind-altering anxiety. The same that tore through me when I was standing over any number of deceased humans, the tragedy I had encountered for what was essentially my entire adult life.

After our brief introduction and initial rundown as to why I was there was out of the way, I felt my anxiety lessening as she talked. "John, I will do whatever I can to help you. And I will not rush things."

"Thank you," was about all I could mumble. Who knew more than myself that a mental-health condition has no timeline, something many people seem to think it must have.

The rest of the session was about establishing a rapport and making small talk. As I felt it, the idea was to not only get to know one another, but to determine what therapeutic direction to take.

When the forty-five-minute session came to its end, I booked my next appointment, said my goodbyes, and headed for the parking lot. Once in my car, I felt so mentally exhausted that I had to wait before going home. I just closed my eyes...and let the years in the fire service flash through my mind like an episode of heat lightning flashing randomly through the night sky. "I can't do this," I whispered to myself.

When I finally made the five-minute trip home, I could feel myself cutting off from the outside world. No more hellish torment or the world thrusting me into an emergency situation, one I would be powerless to help with. Once that door closed behind me, I felt a feeling of safety come over me.

But my long battle to get to the point of recurring psychological treatment had taken a massive toll on what little strength remained. So, once I got home from day one of therapy, I collapsed. Like someone stranded at sea once rescued, I felt the remaining strength leave my body, instantly making me aware of how exhausted I was. All I could do was hide from the world and spend several days sleeping or remaining idle. I needed the silence.

A Marathon, Not a Race

In the coming weeks and months, I would find myself in a rare, long-lasting, yet low-grade stint of stability. I had a structured routine. Now I had a great balance of therapeutic skill-building and peace, having many hours alone at home. As my partner went to work every day, I was able to pace myself throughout my everyday life. When I was near crisis, there were little or no obstacles to take time to reboot. I was able to customize the way I lived my life, for the first time.

Each session with the psychologist brought a small measure of success and, at times, setbacks. Tackling those deep-seated psychological injuries can be exhausting and because of this, I was often written off for the remainder of the day afterwards.

Although I resigned myself to the fact that the exploration of PTSD's debilitating power was painful and raw and thus very mentally taxing, I rarely let it fester past one day. In fact, I was and still remain headstrong, and still talk to myself, like one persona reassuring the other. "I am determined to keep building on a plan that will see the shackles of mental illness release me from its grasp!" Giving power to that voice helps.

When I look back at the beginning of my battle with post-traumatic stress disorder, I remember comparing it to my experiences tackling my generalized anxiety disorder. This turned out to be a naive notion on my part. PTSD is nothing like generalized anxiety disorder. Nothing. Anxiety's punch has the force of a toddler. PTSD is like a prized MMA fighter. It can leave you flat on your back in seconds, before you know what hit you. In my view, it's the heavyweight champion of all anxiety disorders.

I was able to draw from my old healing handbook, and diet and exercise have helped tremendously – but do little to quell the nightmares, flashbacks and sleepless nights that come standard with PTSD. No matter how hard I've tried, I can't outrun the roll of film that runs on the imaginary spools that force me to relive my fire-service and long term-care days.

Because it was and still is very debilitating, I realize I am playing a long game, one I can't afford to let up on. As it became clear to me that I was disabled by my trauma, I knew I had to add to my existing mental-health team, while at the same time finding some way to cope outside of the mental-health supports. "Know your enemy," I often say to myself, "And you can defeat it.".

Armed with this knowledge, I committed to being open to anything and everything, Even medication. "You moved away from pills years ago and that was fine," I said to myself. "Fine as long as you kept up the healthy living. Yeah, I know, you were able to manage anxiety's symptoms without it. But this is a different ball game. It comes harder and faster, and that's just a grain of it." The symptoms of PTSD are excruciating and so much so that I said "yes" to every pharmaceutical option being offered by my psychiatrist. I told her, "I hate medication, but the pain is so tough, I'm willing to try anything you think will help."

As my luck would have it, my other lifelong illness, epilepsy, would play a role in derailing all the drug's chemical properties used to treat mental illness. It was not the disease itself, but rather the medication I was on to control the seizures. Turns out, this anti-convulsant flushed out all the drugs she prescribed, out of my liver, rendering them useless and leaving me struggling to cope with the symptoms of not only PTSD, but the depressive disorder too.

I felt frustrated, yeah. But I was so desperate to end the pain and get back to living that I was willing to keep working with her to – I hoped – find a drug that would steer this worn and tired old ship in the right direction.

The Big Stall

To complicate matters, many of the medications I tried ended up derailing other aspects of my wellness plan. After fighting for years to get back to a healthy weight and a more mentally-well self, I willingly put that in jeopardy. In that moment it was a risk I was willing to take. I just wanted the nightmares and hyper-vigilance to end. Pain regardless of its source, mental or physical, if left long enough, can eventually be too powerful to tolerate.

Many of these medications cause weight gain and sure enough, I would turn out to be one of the unlucky ones who put on many pounds. Five years of backbreaking work dissolved in the matter of a few months. Every week my belly seemed to be a bit rounder, and I felt a bit more winded, something that was really apparent when I did exercise. Personally, I was disappointed, but I kept telling myself, "You've gotten in shape before, and you can do it again."

I'd like to say it was worth it and it would have been, had one or more of the medications worked – but as is the case in many gambles in life, you win some, you lose some. I didn't only lose, I suffered a monumental setback. Now, to go with all the mental pain, I had an unhealthy dose of low self-esteem, was sedated all the time, and couldn't get out of my own way. Every four to six weeks, the conversation with the psychiatrist went something like; "John, how is the new med working out?"

My reply was always the same. "I am feeling no different other than being so doped up, I am sleeping so much. I don't consider being knocked out all the time as progress."

Not only was this attempt at pharmaceutical intervention a colossal failure in terms of helping me manage my illnesses, but the side effects hit me hard. I was sedated to the point that I couldn't drive. At times, I felt as though I could sleep standing up. All these medications did was eat away at my already-limited and precious time I had with family. I had gotten to know only the hardships of the evil side of these pills and none of the benefits that many people have.

That was my reality: that my quality of life was further damaged by the many months of exploration with meds designed to quiet my mind. I felt even further isolated. As if that weren't enough, the chemically-induced exhaustion, depending on the drug, made me feel like I was trying to run through the ocean. Every moment was a struggle. Finally, six months into this experiment, my psychiatrist decided that everything that could be done to help from a medical point of view had been done. "I... we have done all we can do. I don't know what else to say to you, but to continue to live each day as it comes. And you have the resources we have given you."

While I did manage to have some minimal benefit from some meds, I closed this chapter of my life, discouraged. Her efforts to help, great as they had been, only stalled my healing journey. I was too stoned to do anything but crawl.

This had an impact on the therapist's attempts. Not knowing whether I was coming or going made it hugely difficult to participate in her attempts to make a dent in my struggle. She spent a lot of time teaching me mindfulness techniques: "Try to feel your feet on the floor and call attention to where you're feeling your angst and fear. Breathe, in through the nose and out through the mouth."

I tried. However, I spent the majority of the sessions fighting with my eyelids to stay open. With eyes heaving and burning, I turned my naps in the parking lot afterwards into a part of the routine.

With that said, we did make tiny but observable improvements. I was learning to be more "in the moment," and this helped me fight off the pain of trauma and the dread of anxiety when alone, but was useless in public. The noise and commotion still wreaked havoc with me. The busy-ness of the outside world overtook me faster than I could apply the coping tools I was being taught.

A plate hitting the floor, a sudden roar of laughter from a neighbouring table, would be enough to cause an involuntary mental shock that went at light-speed throughout my entire body, bringing me off my feet or out of my chair. Hyper-vigilance is a special kind of torture, especially when being scared out of one's skin repeatedly in a public setting. It was like getting a low-level electric shock over and over. Totally beyond my control, it had a residual effect that produced a whole gamut of emotions. First, fear, then a strong sense of urgency to run, followed by an accumulation of real anger.

And then there are the social repercussions of this "startle response." I once jumped out of my chair in a café, ready for action because a young lady probably in her early twenties had dropped her aluminum water-bottle on the ceramic tiled floor. "Oh, my God!" I apologized profusely but the terror in her eyes was heartbreaking. I still choke up over that one.

There were moments when the thought of ending my life seemed like an effective solution to this torture. Would I have the guts to do it? But I fought on because I needed to, because I want to.

Suicide sometimes seems like a sensible solution. I know that it's not – however, pain is pain and the longer one goes without any real relief, it starts to make sense. "I can't stand it, but, alas, I will fight on!"

What ultimately fuels my desire to keep moving forward is the realization that I am one of many with a vested interest in my life. My parents, my sister, my children, and close friends also have an emotional investment in my well-being and therefore, I keep on. Out of all the pain and discomfort, I know I have a lot to be grateful for. It's also very evident that I am loved, dearly. For that, you remain committed to all those who provide you with connection and the little joy you may have in life.

CHAPTER NINETEEN

Rescue the Rescuer

"There's no shame in your mental pain. You can come back from your own darkness."

Purpose keeps me going. I've known that for a long time. It's partly that little fellow inside me, what I call the inner child, the one who always wanted "idealistic." Purpose is how I became such an advocate for mental illness/wellness, even an "influencer," as some people have suggested.

I'm a skilled counsellor, if not a certified one. I'm (sometimes) a whiz with tech and social media. And I've learned the huge difference exercise – running and dripping sweat and pounding heart – makes. I also have two young people in my life, my son and daughter, who I live for.

Which doesn't explain the day that I finally decided "Enough is enough!" and stuffed some clothes and things in a backpack and threw it in the back of my brand-new Toyota-Corolla Hybrid. I was heading off to end it all, i.e., to kill myself. And you might have thought it was some kind of morbid celebration. I did feel lighter. Hadn't worked out all the details yet. But I got in, turned the key, and drove off to meet my maker, or whatever might be in its place.

"Is there anything that can rescue this veteran rescuer?" I'd thought for a long time. I'd been fighting this for years. You can't imagine how tired I was – unless, wait, maybe you can – if you've been through this mental-illness hell. I just didn't see much on the horizon, in spite of all the "positives" I rolled out in the first paragraph. So I went driving along, feeling George Michael's ballad about being loved, just ripping through me. Seconds after that, it would happen...fate with a purpose.

But until then, I'd been reflecting. "I know I can get there" I can say, or at least on the days when the darkness lifts, just enough to bring me some relief. I often feel, or know, good days are fewer and fewer, bad days are more and more intense. How can it be otherwise when you can feel trapped by the everyday routines of everyone walking, running and driving by you; a burst of laughter here, a dropping of dishes there? PTSD's "startle" response is a special kind of hell.

I often describe it to people like this: "Imagine someone has a low-level taser. Now, imagine them zapping you with it ten times minimum a day. That's kinda what it's like to have your fight-or-flight always in gear. Everything makes you jump."

This is where I'm at, despite being that advocate, counsellor, devoted father. Can't handle noise, large crowds – hell, I can't even handle a car passing me on the highway. "Everything feels like a goddamn threat!" I've yelled. Nearly every therapy session, this line comes out somewhere within the 45-minute sit-down.

To the nightmares and inexplicable bursts of anger, add a dash of "Can you please turn down the music?" when out at a cafe or other public space. And what I'm left with is a severely customized life with a very limited ability to go the distance in social settings.

"Damn it, why can't the world just be quieter, flex for me more often?" It's much, much more than the "stress" caused by an overly-loud world for most people.

I'm left feeling full of dread, sadness, and regret for all the personal sacrifices I've made in the name of helping my community. "I'm also angry, pissed off that I can't seem to break out of the shackles of PTSD. In fact, it's so tough to negotiate the wider world, fuelled by the fires of my depressive disorder." Yup, I'm still talking to myself.

We've been down the road on meds in this book, and I know they're the reality for a lot of us. But oh, how, for me, they only fill in the dark with fog in an attempt to quell the suicidal ideation – and manage to exhaust me before noon most days. "I'm tired." I find these words forcing themselves out of my lips more and more as of late. Most days, I am uncertain about how much more of mental illness's brutality I can take.

Every day when I wake, one of the first things I do is think about my psychologist and how grateful I am to have her and her professional guidance. Because of her I can get out with friends for short periods, and I can manage low-level stimulus. Without her, that could never be possible. But "perhaps you have hit your ceiling for getting better?" she once said while I was in her office, battling a particularly bad depressive episode.

While tiny gatherings may seem 'too small' to many, I have come to love and appreciate them. They are huge for me and offer a sliver of light into the parts of me locked up by fear.

Just Wanting the Pain to End

As the years have rolled by, it becomes more about not wanting something to happen – but for something to end. That's why I have been fighting all my adult life, looking for that magic pain reliever. Apparently, it doesn't exist, at least not for me.

I have said to many, especially in the last few months that "when I think about suicide, it feels good." In a depressive state or traumatic episode, it starts to make sense. It is not an easy way out as is often suggested. It's a massive wrestle for the knife to save oneself, constantly. With that said, I am proud that I have a huge support system, a network of kind people who have saved me every time.

Just two weeks ago I was determined to put the pain to rest. They only way to do that was to lay me to rest too. So to speak. I knew the car, my brand-new Toyota Corolla Hybrid, would be part of it.

The day I decided "enough is enough," I was so full of dread, it felt as though someone had dropped the entire ocean on my head, I was existing in cement shoes and just said "I'm done!" Retrieving my black, multi-pocketed backpack, I calmly filled it with some clothes – a t-shirt, jeans, a sweater. I thought, "Just in case I don't jump off a cliff on the hike I had planned, I will stay at a hotel and see if the quiet offers something" – as I have had in the past in such a room. When the world became too much, my nervous system needed the sweet sound of silence.

Looking back on that day, I am struck by just how calm I was. My movements were slowed, my plan was all but certain, and I felt a rare kind of peace wash over me. I needed this pain to stop! As I tossed the backpack into my new 2021 Hybrid, I took one last look at my mom and dad's house, said, "I love you guys," jumped in, started the car, and headed west. The drive...there was something about it that felt, well, not memorable, considering the purpose. "Like, what did I lease this brand-new car for?" How ridiculous, to have it for a couple of weeks before I said goodbye. But I was clinging to "No more noise, no more living scared and no more visions of a young man, lying lifeless on the front porch of my aunt's apartment." All these things whizzed through my head as I got closer to my destination. Depression has its own script, its own agenda. I would feel different again, after that overcast morning.

Serendipity – with a Purpose

As I entered the final small Nova Scotian town, the last before my final destination, I was at peace, like all the mindfulness and meditating in the world had been gifted to me from all those who practice them. Oh, what a feeling! And as I rolled by the semi-familiar buildings that lined either side of the main street, I was listening to George Michael's beautiful ballad about being loved, a song he wrote after the loss of his partner and the death of his mother. I remember thinking, "Man, I know those who love me will be devastated, but they don't know the pain I am in."

Mere seconds after the last line, about being loved, burst from the car's brand new eight, front-to-back speakers, I was jarred by a sudden clunk. Out of nowhere, my first thought was, "Oh God, I hit a kid."

The sound of the back fender crumbling was so unexpected that all I remember was a total feeling of confusion. "What the hell!" I said as I slowly made my way to the curb. Because I thought I had hit something, I bounced out of the driver seat in time to see an older Chrysler 300 also pulling over to the curb. An older man got out and said, "Are you alright?

"Yes," I said "Yes, I'm okay."

I was so convinced that I had hit something, that I said, "What did I hit?" Before the tall, grey-haired retired pharmacist (I somehow took all that in) could answer, I could see his front right fender and hood were buckled up.

I remember him saying, "I think they can bang that out. How's your car?" We looked. The light-grey rear fender on the driver's side was lightly buckled and scratched. The scratches ran from just before the back door and over the right side of the bumper.

"Oh, that doesn't look bad," I said. But a closer look revealed that the back control arm had been snapped.

All in all, the interaction between this gentle-spoken man and myself was positive and cooperative. We took the time to exchange insurance information and made small talk for a bit. What sticks out the most for me was how calm and unfazed I was about it. It was as though I was giving him my phone number to go for coffee or something.

Because my car was so new, I had not yet received the insurance cards, so I was trying frantically to find the information required to pass along to him. Then it dawned on me that I had TD insurance's phone number on my phone, so I started to thumb through my Google contact list on my LG mobile. As my attention was centred on digging up the number, I was only partially aware of my surroundings and I just blurted out, "Well, it's not all bad, you hitting me. You saved my life. I was going to kill myself today."

His eyes widened and he stared at me. After a moment he said, "Nothing can be that bad that you need to commit suicide. Life is worth living."

I said, "Well, I have PTSD and it's just too much. I just want the pain over with."

"You in the military?" he asked.

"Nope, fifteen years in the fire service," I said.

"Oh," he said. "That would be difficult."

Once I had spilled my guts about my plans for that day, there was an awkward silence. "Well, I better get home and call my insurance company, so please, take care." he said.

"You too, and please, hang in there."

"I will, and good luck."

If it were any other day, this accident would have been met with a "pain in the ass" kind of response. Calling the tow truck, being stuck in a town where I had no friends, would have made my anger fester, but I remained in a state of melancholy, from the beginning to the end.

But it did save my life. A sign? Maybe. However, you see it, it's an opportunity to have a new start. "John, you gotta keep going, you have so many great people in your life," I tell myself, then "I want to live, and I want to see happier times."

On that day, no one was hurt, and cars can be replaced or repaired, but with life it's different. That early afternoon, I wrote myself off, but evidently, I still have some work here to do. While it wasn't a revelation, and didn't cure my PTSD or wipe away depression and anxiety, it did give me a second chance.

Today, I am still suffering. I have been sleeping night and day, but I keep telling myself, "This too shall pass." And you know what? It always does. And, isn't that what life is? Making it through the tough moments and living to soak up every happy moment, breathing in the laugh with a good friend, a hug from your children and the support from those who care.

I know that PTSD and depression will always be part of me, but despite it, I have so much living to do. I will probably always be that advocate and counsellor, and have more people in my life because of my illness. But whatever I do, I will survive this. We can survive this.

"Remember, regardless of how limited your energy is, you still have a choice of where to put it. Find your new passion, allow it to be your purpose and live through the pain to feel those moments of joy."

Jonathan Arenburg

ABOUT THE AUTHOR

Jonathan Arenburg is a mental health blogger, writer, speaker, wellness coach and published author; He is also the host of the mental wellness podcast, #thewellnesstalks.

He has also appeared in the *i'Mpossible's Lemonade Stand III*. He has also been a contributing writer for "Mental Health Talk," a column in his local paper. In addition, he has also written for the mental health advocacy organization; Sick Not Weak.

Jonathan has also appeared on several mental health-related podcasts, including: A New Dawn, The Depression Files, Books and Authors, and Men Are Nuts. He is a returning panellist for the Bipolar Girl Podcast and regularly consults with LEAD, a mental health and coaching organization in Nigra, Africa.

Since being put off work because of PTSD, Jonathan has dedicated his time to his mental wellness journey while helping others along the way.

Educated as an addictions' counsellor, he has dedicated most of his professional life of eighteen years, working with those who have intellectual disabilities, behavioural challenges, and mental illness.

He has also spent fifteen years in the volunteer fire service helping his community.

His book, *The Road to Mental Wellness*, goes into detail about his life-long battle with depression, anxiety and more recently, PTSD. In it, he hopes to provide insight on how mental illness cultivates over a lifetime and, if not recognized and treated, how it impacts the entirety of one's life; right from childhood into the adult years. Jonathan lives with his two children in Nova Scotia, Canada.

CONNECT WITH THE AUTHOR

Twitter: @ArenburgJohn

Email: *johnnixona@gmail.com*

Blog: *theroadtomentalwellness.com*

Blog email: *roadtomentalwellness@gmail.com*

Podcast: Host of #thewellnesstalks

Want to be on the show? Email us: thewellnesstalkspodcast@gmail.com

***

Reviews, good or bad, are important to authors. Please leave one if you have a moment. Thank you.

***

Know someone who would like to read this book? Buy a copy(s) by using your phone to scan the QR code below.

Manufactured by Amazon.ca
Bolton, ON